REFUGEE EDUCATION:
MAPPING THE FIELD

REFUGEE EDUCATION: MAPPING THE FIELD

Edited by Crispin Jones and Jill Rutter

Trentham Books

First published in 1998 by Trentham Books Limited

Reprinted 2001

Trentham Books Limited
Westview House
734 London Road
Oakhill
Stoke on Trent
Staffordshire
England ST4 5NP

British Cataloguing in Publication Data
A catalogue record for this book is available from the British Library
ISBN 1 85856 055 1

Cover photograph: © Tim Fox

Designed and typeset by Trentham Print Design Ltd., Chester and printed in Great Britain by The Cromwell Press Ltd., Wiltshire

CONTENTS

Acknowledgements • vi

The Authors • vii

Chapter 1
**Mapping the Field:
Current Issues in Refugee Education** • 1
Crispin Jones and Jill Rutter

Chapter 2
Refugees in Today's World • 13
Jill Rutter

Chapter 3
**Refugees, Asylum Seekers and the Housing Crisis:
No Place to Learn** • 33
Sally Power, Geoff Whitty and Deborah Youdell

Chapter 4
Unaccompanied – but not Unsupported • 49
Louise Williamson

Chapter 5
The Psychological Adaptation of Refugee Children • 75
William Yule

Chapter 6
Supporting Refugee Children in the Early Years • 93
Tina Hyder

Chapter 7
**Supporting Refugee Children in East London
Primary Schools** • 107
Bill Bolloten and Tim Spafford

Chapter 8
**Working with Refugee Children:
One School's Experience** • 125
Caroline Lodge

Chapter 9
**Refugee Students' Experiences of the UK
Education System** • 149
Jeremy McDonald

Chapter 10
The Educational Needs of Refugee Children • 171
Crispin Jones

Bibliography • 183

Index • 193

ACKNOWLEGEMENTS

Over the last few years, the Institute of Education's Refugee Education Initiative has been organising evening seminars on refugee education. The seminars have been well attended, mainly by London teachers, and have covered a wide range of topics. Members of the Refugee Education Initiative believe that the topics raised and discussed in these seminars deserve a wider audience and this book is the result.

We are grateful to all the authors who so readily agreed to write for this volume. In addition, we owe a particular debt of gratitude to our colleagues, Ann Gold, Jagdish Gundara and Charlie Owen, who have been prime movers in getting this Initiative up and running. We would also like to thank all those refugee children who recounted their experiences to the authors of this book.

This book is dedicated to Audrey Moser in recognition of her work for refugee children.

Crispin Jones and Jill Rutter
January 1998

THE AUTHORS

Bill Bolloten is a Refugee Support Teacher in the London Borough of Newham.

Tina Hyder is the co-ordinator of the Equality Learning Centre, Save the Children.

Crispin Jones is a Senior Lecturer in Education at the Institute of Education, University of London, working in the International Centre for Intercultural Studies.

Caroline Lodge was the headteacher of George Orwell School, Islington from 1989 until 1995, when she moved to the Institute of Education, University of London, working in the National Professional Qualification Centre as head of the Training and Development Centre.

Jeremy McDonald is a Research Officer in the Post 16 Education Centre at the Institute of Education, University of London.

Sally Power, formerly in the Health and Education Research Unit at the Institute of Education is now a Lecturer in Education at the University of Bristol.

Jill Rutter is National Education Adviser at the Refugee Council and Research Officer, Refugee Education Initiative at the Institute of Education, University of London, working in the International Centre for Intercultural Studies.

Tim Spafford is a Refugee Support Teacher in the London Borough of Newham.

Geoff Whitty is Karl Mannheim Professor of the Sociology of Education and head of the Health and Education Research Unit at the Institute of Education.

Louise Williamson was Director of the Children's Division at the Refugee Council until 1997.

Deborah Youdell works in the Health and Education Research Unit at the Institute of Education.

William Yule is Professor of Applied Child Psychology at the Institute of Psychiatry, University of London.

CHAPTER ONE

Mapping the Field: Current Issues in Refugee Education

Crispin Jones and Jill Rutter

I was so enthusiastic about starting school and learning English. I had been away from school for two years because we were travelling and did not have a permanent place to live. I promised myself not to miss school again and not to waste more time. I had to be serious and work hard, there was no time for being lazy. Ten days after my arrival I started going to a school close to my house.

The problem was at my age I should have been doing A-Levels, but because I didn't speak English they put me in Year Ten with students who were three years younger than me. The teachers didn't believe I would be able to do GCSEs with so little English. I was told that the best thing for me was to stay in Year Ten until my English was better and maybe in two years I could attempt some GCSEs.

Being with younger people is not a problem if they are mature. But when you are a teenager a three year difference is quite a big gap, especially if you don't speak the language and are new to the culture. It is at this time that you need friends the most. But I was shocked to find out that in the lunch queue they used to laugh at me and say that I never had decent food in my country. They said I had always been hungry and that's why I ran away from my home. Some people treated me like a fool because I couldn't speak English well, some just ignored me as if I didn't exist.

Nobody wanted to sit next to me in lessons and no-one wanted to have me as their partner in PE. I was all alone in the corner. I did not understand the jokes during the lessons. I couldn't understand the subjects we studied because of my English and could never express myself during any simple discussion. I was too scared to talk because I knew if I made a mistake some of them would laugh at me. Once I even got beaten up by a group of students who used to bully everyone. They beat me up one evening when I was walking home alone. They said they couldn't stand me because I was a refugee who lived on the Government's money (which they considered to be their own money). After this I lost all my confidence... I almost gave up. The reason that I didn't was because of my mother's help and the support I got from my teachers and a school charity. (Testimony of a Kurdish refugee student, who eventually went on to university. From Rutter, 1996)

There are over 46,000 refugee children and young people in UK schools and colleges in 1998. But the sad fact is that the current state of play in respect of the refugee students in schools and colleges is not satisfactory. It is also a fact that refugee students are not a problem for the education system. Their presence in the schools and colleges of this country does, however, reveal problems that have always been there within the education system itself. In this introductory chapter, we draw out some of the more important issues raised for education by refugee students and indicate some of the themes that are considered in greater detail in subsequent chapters of this book. We are aware that the field that we map, namely refugee education, is not only very large, it is very old too. And forcing the metaphor somewhat, we are equally aware that the map that this book presents is no more than an outline and that much work remains to be done if the field is to be adequately understood.

Refugee students are about as old as education itself in the English context. If one talks about mass rather than elite education, their presence is even clearer. Mass education in Britain is an urban phenomenon which can readily be traced back to the 16th century (Bash et al., 1984). Running alongside this is a continual refugee presence, from Huguenot refugees in the Spitalfields area of London in the 16th century to the range of refugee groups that have been a feature of 20th century English education. Indeed, the mosque in Spitalfields' Brick Lane is a fascinating monument to the refugee presence in London. First built as a Huguenot church, the same building became successively an Anglican church, a centre for the Anglican mission for the conversion of the Jews, a synagogue and is currently a mosque. Against this spiritual message of change and continuity, has to be put an uglier history of xenophobia, antisemitism and racism that have disfigured the same area of London, epitomised by the anti-fascist Battle of Cable Street in 1936. But throughout this history, the various refugee groups have attempted to ensure that their children gain an education that will ensure their success in the new society that has, with varying degrees of reluctance, given them shelter (e.g. Bash, 1995).

Despite this history, it is easy to slip into a perspective that sees refugee children as a problem. A busy inner city primary teacher may have a class that is full of children with special educational needs, bilingual children whose access to the curriculum is being limited by their English language competence and other children whose commitment to learning appears minimal or remote. Resources to meet these multifarious needs are never sufficient and it only needs an impending government OFSTED inspection to make the teacher wonder why their particular career choice was ever made. Put an unheralded, non-English speaking refugee child into that teacher's classroom on a wet, cold February Monday morning and a camel's-last-straw reaction may seem understandable. However, talking to many such teachers over the last few years, we have come to appreciate that this initial and unconsidered reaction – if it occurs – seldom lasts long. Most teachers who have refugee students in their classes do not see them as problem students. Individual refugee students, like individual non-refugee students, may have various learning and other educational difficulties and needs, but refugee students also bring into the classroom a range of opportunities and perspectives that can enrich the learning and understandings of everyone working there.

So if refugee students have the potential to bring positive elements into classrooms, what are the barriers that prevent that potential from being revealed and utilised? Are there sets of educational needs that are

3

common to refugee students? If there are, how best may they be met? In light of the evidence that we have collected (Jones, 1993; LBGCRE, 1994; Rutter, 1994), there do seem to be issues that face many, but by no means all, refugee students. The chapters in this book offer a range of potential answers to those questions. In this chapter, to help frame the work of the remaining contributors, we highlight a number of the major issues as we currently perceive them.

We begin with an examination of the political and social factors which affect the settlement and education of asylum-seeking and refugee children. The last ten years have seen increasingly restrictive asylum legislation introduced all across Europe. Potential asylum-seekers now see their route to safety blocked by the imposition of visa requirements and by the use of carrier sanctions fining airlines and other carriers who transport the undocumented (see Cruz, 1995). Asylum-seekers have seen their social rights restricted, as part of a policy of 'humane deterrence' (as termed by Kenneth Clark when Home Secretary in 1992). Most drastically the Asylum and Immigration Act 1996 restricted most asylum-seekers' access to benefits. And fewer and fewer asylum-seekers are eventually recognised as refugees under the terms of the 1951 UN Convention and 1967 Protocol Relating to the Status of Refugees. The impact of these legislative changes is discussed in greater depth in Chapter Two, but as a result asylum-seeking and refugee children are now

- likely to be living in conditions of continual stress caused by uncertainty about their future, thus compounding possible trauma experienced in the home country;

- likely to be living in various forms of temporary accommodation and likely to be very mobile as a result;

- more likely to be attending unpopular schools in the local authority, because of their mobility.

So it is not surprising that refugee students tend to come into contact with the educational system at its most under-resourced and stretched. Despite a general hostility, asylum-seekers continue to arrive in the UK from other parts of Europe and the rest of the world. The most significant groups currently come from eastern Europe and the Horn of

Africa. 'Significance' in this context relates to politics and media rather than actual numbers. In the period since 1970, the numerically significant groups of refugees in the UK have been from Uganda, Cyprus, Vietnam, Iran, Sri Lanka, Somalia, former Yugoslavia, Kurds from Iran, Iraq and Turkey, Nigerians and Zaireans. The majority, some 90 per cent, stay in the London area, where they have supportive networks, as evidenced by the numbers of refugee community organisations found there. Of some 214 such organisations identified in a research study in 1995, only 23 were outside London (IOE/MORI, 1995). One consequence of this concentration is that refugee school students are a significant presence in the capital's schools, some 39,000 in 1997 (Refugee Council, 1997). However, despite their numbers, their pattern of migration and settlement can result in the refugees leading quite isolated and economically marginal lives. Currently in London, for example, there is considerable concern for Somali refugees, particularly over their marginality, high unemployment and the inability of the usual social agencies to assist them.

More generally, however, despite their individual distribution across the city, refugees' overall concentration in inner London has led to their subsequent concentration in specific schools. But it can be quite difficult to write about specific schools that have significant numbers of refugee students because there is a quite widely held view, that schools with large numbers of refugee and asylum seeking students are frequently seen as not just under-subscribed but, more damagingly, as failing schools – a view most certainly not held in this book.

Refugee school students in London do indeed tend to attend under-subscribed schools. There are several reasons for this. Under-subscribed schools are the ones with vacant places; they are therefore schools to which Local Education Authorities [LEAs] often direct refugee and asylum seeking school students, knowing that a place will be available. LEAs and other agencies will also direct refugee and asylum seeking parents and school students to such schools on the grounds that they already have other refugee school students who can give support to the newcomers, as well as teachers who are accustomed to the special demands that the refugee children might make upon the education system. Furthermore, schools which have a reputation

5

among refugee communities for being supportive will obviously attract more such students. Such schools, certainly the majority of those visited in the course of our recent work, were justifiably proud of their successes with refugee students and also, equally importantly, aware of their failures.

Whether having a large number of such students makes such schools more popular with the non-refugee population is open to question, given the hostility that most refugees face in this country. Consequently, many refugee students, a particularly vulnerable group of school students, attend schools which are under-subscribed, often unpopular and usually having a greater proportion of other children who make heavy demands upon the teachers' time and skills, for example in relation to English as an Additional Language [EAL] needs. Such schools are unlikely to appear high up in the current government's crude league tables, although the value added education that many provide would lead to some surprises if a more subtle, fair and comprehensive system of school evaluation were to be adopted.

A further adverse factor is that, by their very nature, refugees do not fit into the tidy pattern of the school year that starts in September and ends the following July. Formerly called 'casual admissions' term time admissions of refugees [and, of course, other children] are the norm rather than the exception in some schools. Classes are constantly changing: new students appear and others disappear. The disruption this causes and the extra demands on teachers to welcome, reassure and effectively educate the newcomers and the rest of the class should not be underestimated. Under such circumstances induction becomes a continuous process rather than a carefully organised event for Year Seven in September. It requires careful planning and implementation for a continuous induction policy to ensure that refugee children have an easy and successful transition into the life of the school, a point that is taken up later on in this chapter and elsewhere in this book.

All this means that schools that are already under pressure are placed under yet more. A cynic could say that each LEA needs such a school, an unpopular, under-subscribed school, where it can place pupils with great learning needs, so as to enable the other schools to concentrate on improving their published exam scores. Such students, the disruptive, those with learning needs that are unsupported by statements of special educational needs, bilingual students – the list is a long one – are generally no longer wanted by secondary schools that are full. Many secondary schools now prefer such students to be elsewhere. And for so long as the efforts made with such children are not recognised in published league tables, the schools who do have them will be seen to be unsuccessful.

This is not to say that under-subscribed schools are always seen as failing schools – this is clearly not the case. Nor that there are no unsuccessful, under-subscribed schools – they do exist. And we are definitely not saying that schools with a good many refugee students are likely to be failing. We are arguing that schools with many refugee children often do well by them but that this is seldom recognised by the education service in general. During our research we encountered a refugee student who had returned to the school he had originally started at, after his family moved him to another school they thought was 'better', which in league table terms it was. He spent a term at the new school before returning, because he believed that his educational needs, academic and pastoral, were better met at his original school. Yes, there was a more academic atmosphere at the second school but his English language needs were barely touched upon; there was a pastoral system but he felt that his classmates, unlike those in his original school, did not really understand the reasons why there were refugee students in the school or why there were refugees in that part of London at all.

This example touches on two of the major issues, namely providing adequate language support that enables refugee students to fulfil their academic potential and giving all students information and understandings about refugees that encourages sympathetic perceptions and tolerance and helps oppose frequently found xenophobia. Other issues that teachers need to tackle are the induction of refugee children into a new education system and the requirement to meet refugee children's psychosocial and emotional needs.

Refugee students are not the only bilingual students in schools and colleges. In inner London, as in other major urban centres in England, there are frequently more bilingual students in schools than monolingual ones. This has been a feature of such areas for many years now but the educational needs that this fact implies are seldom adequately met. EAL support is largely funded by Section 11 of the Local Government Act 1966. This was originally seen as a short term measure by the then Government but it still remains the major source of funding for EAL teaching. Although the major source, nobody would argue that it is adequate for the need. The education system still has to face up to the fact that bilingual students always have been and will continue to be a common feature of urban schools. The implications of this are clear. Mainstream teachers need in-service training and support if they are to meet the needs of their bilingual students. Many inner city LEAs recognise this but have few resources to meet the needs. Central government, using various sources of money, mostly the Grants for Educational Support and Training [GEST], has attempted to give support but the sums of money are totally inadequate. And initial teacher education still gives too little attention to this area, meaning newly-qualified teachers are still coming into multilingual schools without any idea about how they might support their bilingual students' learning. A straw poll of newly qualified teachers in Tower Hamlets, a London Borough with an extremely high number of bilingual students, found that only a quarter had done work in this area during their training. In particular, there needs to be an improvement in the way that English language support is given to refugee children who have a severely interrupted or non-existent prior education [an issue faced by many children who have fled from war zones where schools have closed]. Quality teaching materials and strategies for such children are few and far between.

Within this context, refugee children merely re-emphasise the need for better provision. On top of the other difficulties they may be facing in British society, being denied access to the mainstream curriculum because of language support is inadequate is another burden that they could well do without. As for any form of support for their first language, the position is even bleaker. Despite EU directives in the area of language support, the English education system remains, in the main, wedded to a view of the learning of languages that reflects the power of the monolingual English. Refugee students highlight such issues but this has still done little for them. This is not to demean the huge efforts that are made by some schools and local authorities: it is more a matter of stating too little and often too late.

Language difficulties are, in a sense, a technical matter which could readily be solved if adequate resources were made available. Other difficulties are less easy to deal with. Two in particular stand out here, namely, countering anti-refugee feelings in schools and adequately dealing with the range of issues raised by refugee students whose previous experiences have caused severe emotional and physical trauma. [They are considered in greater detail later in the book.]

Anti-refugee sentiment in schools is alive, active and well. It flourishes alongside other forms of racism, xenophobia and narrow nationalism. It is becoming clearer that such feelings amongst school and college students are more complex than was previously thought but strategies are also emerging for helping combat racist activities among young people (CME, 1992; ICIS, 1995). For refugee students, being the victims of such behaviours is doubly damaging, if it is possible to make useful gradations in relation to this area. Fleeing forms of violence and oppression, they may again face similar behaviours just when they think they have reached some form of asylum. All racism is harmful and should be firmly dealt with by schools. More than that, all students need to be taught about racism, how it is reproduced, whose interests it serves and how it may be rejected and opposed. Many schools still find this a difficult task, made no easier by a social climate in which the issue is seen as 'political' and therefore an inappropriate concern for schools and colleges.

The difficulties that arise from trauma are equally complex. Not all refugee students have experienced overwhelming loss and suffering in their home countries and many can process and deal with the complex emotions associated with trauma, loss and change. Teachers are not generally trained and nor do they feel competent to deal with the complex range of issues to which trauma gives rise. However, there is still a great deal that teachers can do, often by developing the already excellent pastoral care systems in place, and this, too, is taken up in more detail later in the book.

The initial few months in a new school in a new country have been identified as a crucial period for young refugee students. Practices need to be in place that make these children and their carers feel welcome in a new school. Children's past educational experiences and current needs must be accurately assessed on arrival. Those who are 14 or older need to be given realistic careers guidance and educational pathways so that they can make informed choices. The issue of induction and initial assessment of pupils is examined in Chapters Seven and Eight.

This book is published at a time of great educational change at both compulsory and post-compulsory level. Most importantly for refugee children, the way that Section 11 funding is administered may change. Section 11 of the Local Government Act 1966 was a source of funding which until 1993 was only available to support communities from the Commonwealth whose language and culture differed from the majority community's. Some 70 per cent of Section 11 money was used to support English language teaching in schools. Most refugee children were theoretically unable to benefit from Section 11 support, because in 1993 only 29 per cent of refugees had their origins in Commonwealth countries. That year the scope of Section 11 funding was broadened so that refugee students from non-Commonwealth countries could benefit directly. Some 14 LEAs have since set up Section 11 funded projects to support refugee children in schools, appointing one or more 'refugee support teachers' to carry out a wide range of tasks to with refugee children. These include supporting individual children who may have needs above and beyond the need to learn English, providing in-service training for schools and helping them in their development of positive policy and practice, making links with a child's home and with refugee communities, and acting as a contact and information point. The work of two refugee support teachers is described in Chapter Seven.

A few LEAs have expanded their refugee support projects within education to include the services of educational psychologists and educational social workers. Such models are judged to be an efficient way of supporting refugee children from a wide range of communities: children who may have complex educational and psychosocial needs. If Section 11 funding is to be changed, it is essential that LEA-based projects for refugee children continue. It is hoped that the ideas described in this book can be used to lobby for effective support for refugee children, which is likely to be currently funded by Section 11.

Finally, as this book was being finished, there was a change of government in Britain. Let us hope that new and more generous ideas in social policy generally and education in particular will give refugee children a better deal in the schools of Britain than they have so far.

CHAPTER TWO

Refugees in Today's World

Jill Rutter

Who are refugees?

There are approximately 46,000 refugee children in British schools (Refugee Council, 1997). They come from a wide range of backgrounds and have many different education and social needs. This chapter examines the causes of refugee movements and Britain's refugee population, especially the possible effects of recent legislative changes on refugee children.

Over 19 million people are refugees in today's world and many others live in refugee-like situations (US Committee for Refugees, 1996). About half of the world's refugees and displaced people are children. The migration of refugees and their reception in host countries is a growing challenge to international agencies, governments, non-governmental organisations and academic institutions. While the vast majority of the world's refugees and displaced people live in poor countries (perhaps over 80 per cent), the refugee population of rich countries has increased since the mid-1980s (see Table 2.1). Asylum policies and the reception of asylum-seekers have become part of the political agenda in western Europe and North America, including the reception of refugees within the education system.

In most educational research about the displaced, the term 'refugee' is used quite loosely. But under international law, the term refugee has a precise meaning. To become a refugee, a person has to be granted refugee status by a host country, having been judged to have 'a well-founded fear of being persecuted for reasons of race, religion, nationality, membership of a particular social group or political opinion' (1951 UN Convention Relating to the Status of Refugees). This definition, framed during the Cold War, excludes people who have fled armed conflict. However, various other international laws, including the European Convention on Human Rights, can be invoked to protect people who have fled armed conflict and are not protected by the 1951 Convention. In Europe for example, the European Convention on Human Rights legislates against return to countries where a person would face cruel, inhuman or degrading treatment. African and Latin American countries have also developed their own treaties to protect those affected by armed conflict. Once refugee status has been granted, persons and their dependants are entitled to remain in their host country indefinitely and also have increased social rights.

Asylum-seekers are those who have crossed international borders in search of safety and refugee status, in another country. In Britain, asylum-seekers are those who are waiting Home Office decisions as to whether they can remain. Asylum applications can be lodged at the port of entry on arrival in Britain, or 'in-country' after a person or family has arrived in Britain.

Table 2.1 Asylum-Seekers in UK 1985-1995

Year	Number
1985	4,389
1986	4,266
1987	4,256
1988	3,998
1989	11,640
1990	26,205
1991	44,840
1992	24,605
1993	22,370
1994	32,830
1995	43,965
1996	29,930

Figures exclude dependants who may not make their own asylum applications.

In Britain about 7 per cent of all asylum-seekers are currently granted refugee status (Home Office, 1996). A further 11 per cent of asylum-seekers are allowed to remain in Britain with another immigration status – that of exceptional leave to remain (ELR). ELR is granted at the discretion of the Home Secretary for 'administrative and humane reasons'. It does not confer the same rights as refugee status; most importantly, it has to be renewed at intervals. Those with ELR also find it more difficult to access grants for further and higher education.

Since 1984 ELR has been granted to an increasing proportion of asylum-seekers. In the past, ELR had been granted to asylum-seekers who were endangered but who fell outside the definition of a refugee outlined in the 1951 UN Convention. A gay man fleeing Iran, or asylum-seekers fleeing a generally unstable and dangerous situation may have been afforded ELR in the past. Today, critics of the British government's asylum policy argue that ELR is now granted to people who would have been afforded refugee status in the early 1980s.

Table 2.2 Asylum Decisions in the UK 1984-1995

	Refugee Status	ELR	Refusal
1984	33	39	28
1985	24	57	19
1986	14	68	18
1987	13	64	23
1988	25	60	15
1989	31	59	10
1990	26	63	11
1991	9	40	51
1992	3	44	53
1993	7	48	46
1994	5	19	76
1995	5	18	77
1996	7	11	81

Figures are percentages

Source: Home Office

An increasing proportion of asylum-seekers are being refused refugee status and leave to remain in Britain. Table 2.2 illustrates this trend. In 1996 some 81 per cent of all asylum-seekers were refused refuge in Britain, including many families with children.

Once notice of refusal of asylum has been granted, an individual's future in the UK becomes increasingly tenuous. That person may appeal, although this may be a financially difficult option. Since the passage of the Asylum and Immigration Act 1996, appellates against asylum decisions are no longer entitled to receive welfare benefits. Those refused asylum may leave Britain voluntarily but may also be removed or deported. A number undoubtedly remain in Britain illegally, part of an urban underclass employed in low paid jobs.

In this chapter the term refugee will be used to describe all those who have fled from persecution, except when it is necessary to describe different immigration statuses. Among 'refugee' students in a British classroom there may be a whole range of immigration statuses: asylum-seekers, those with Convention refugee status, ELR, those appealing against a negative decision and those who have opted to stay in Britain without immigration documentation.

Refugees: casualties of the new world order?
Refugees are very much a product of the conflicts in international, national and regional politics. The reception of refugees in host countries is also influenced by international, national and regional politics. The presence of a refugee child in a classroom reminds us of the existence of such conflicts. If a teacher is to understand the experience of that child, he/she should have some understanding of the international political system into which refugees fit.

There has been a doubling of refugee numbers since 1982 (UNHCR, 1993). Today there are more refugees and internally displaced people than at any other time in history. In the past refugee movements were caused by individual persecution of political opponents or by conflicts between countries over territory. Large scale refugee movements are now primarily caused by conflicts within countries involving a large number of civilians, or 'total warfare'. Of the 30 armed conflicts being fought in today's world according to the Stockholm International Peace

Research Institute (Bellamy, 1996), some 27 are civil wars, being fought within the international boundaries of a country between different ethnic, religious or political groups. Six of these civil wars (in Zaire, Sierra Leone, Liberia, Somalia, Afghanistan and Georgia) have been fought with such intensity that conflict has led to the collapse of effective central government. In these countries public services barely exist outside major urban centres and power lies with local warlords.

While refugees flee in ever greater numbers from civil wars where civilians are the main casualties, the international community seems powerless to prevent such conflicts and is often an ineffective mediator once hostilities erupt. The UN, the organisation set up to maintain peace and the observance of international law, is prevented by its Charter from violating national sovereignty. Where the UN has intervened to prevent conflicts, as in Somalia and Rwanda, it stands accused of incompetence. (In Rwanda in 1994, peacekeeping forces were withdrawn prior to the genocide which left at least one million people dead).

The greatest need of refugees, displaced people and those who are living in ethnic, religious and intercommunal flashpoints, is effective conflict resolution. While conflict resolution involves international diplomacy and disarmament – activities that take place at a macro level – successful conflict resolution must also take place at a local level, within communities. Here there is a role for the education system. Schools and community education can provide a forum for resolving ethnic and religious conflicts and throughout the world there are many examples of such conflict resolution in war zones. For example, much exciting work has been developed in Northern Ireland. In Burundi, UNICEF has funded a theatre project that tours schools and tries to break down long standing prejudices that have led to the conflict between the Tutsi and Hutu communities. But such 'peace education' is badly funded and is often not perceived as real education. Those living in the most stressful circumstances, on the front-line of ethnic or communal conflicts, may not be reached by 'peace education'. But there is a real need for school-based conflict resolution to be properly funded and good practice to be shared internationally.

The lessons of the conflict in the former Yugoslavia must be learned. Some 3.7 million people were forced to flee their homes as refugees or internally displaced people. Some may never return, and may be refugees for the rest of their lives. The conflict witnessed the attempted creation of ethnically pure states. (This is the first time in modern European history since the Nazis that a nation state has attempted to redefine itself as being ethnically pure). It is worth considering the causes of such blatant racism.

Unfortunately, there is no single simple explanation for the bloody war in Bosnia and Croatia and increased tensions in Macedonia and Kosovo. The civil war had its roots in long-standing disputes between ethnic and national groups (Silver, 1995). But other social factors contributed to the outbreak of these wars.

As communist regimes fell across eastern Europe, citizens of former communist countries suffered a *collapse of ideology*. The certainties of life were no longer there. In an ideological void it is easy for populist and nationalist sentiments to flourish: people turn towards that which provides them with certainties. This is what happened throughout the former Yugoslavia. Politicians such as Serbia's Slobodan Milosevic and Croatia's Franjo Tujman deliberately exploited nationalist senti-ments in order to gain support. Politicians encouraged the scapegoating of 'outsiders'. History and culture were manipulated. For example, the standard Croatian language was cleansed of words of supposedly Serbian and Turkish origin. The school curriculum was rewritten. Historical events − such as the bloodshed of the Second World War − were manipulated by different sides of the conflict. Disastrously, there was no strong popular media to challenge this overt nationalism. Television and much of the press were under the control of the nationalists. As the crisis deepened, the economic stresses faced by ordinary people increased. Racism, xenophobia and nationalism all flourish at times of economic hardship. It took little to ignite the Yugoslav tinderbox and cause the flight of millions of people. And conflicts with similar causes happen throughout the world.

Educators are not neutral in such conflicts. Education departments and teachers control school curricula. The curriculum can be used to cause conflict, as happened in Yugoslavia. It can also be used to combat racism, xenophobia and nationalism. In Britain, and in many other parts of the world, there are examples of successful initiatives to counter prejudice (Klein, 1993). Good practice in such prejudice reduction must be funded and shared, but all too often this does not happen.

The New World Order is also that of the free marketeer. Neo-liberal economics have flourished, and public expenditure has been slashed in almost all of the world's countries. European Union countries are now drastically cutting public expenditure in order to meet the economic convergence criteria for monetary union. Consequent public sector cuts affect the refugee in many ways:

- poor and indebted countries have been forced to cut expenditure on health care, education and items such as food subsidies. Structural adjustment policies imposed by the International Monetary Fund and World Bank are often to blame. The poorest suffer and often there is enormous popular discontent after cuts in food subsidies. In many poor countries repression follows discontent, and some of the repressed are forced into exile.

- richer countries have also cut public expenditure, including aid budgets – aid to refugees and also aid to projects that may have helped prevent discontent and mass migration. In Britain, aid was cut from 0.57 per cent of gross national product in 1979 to 0.24 per cent in 1995 (Christian Aid, 1996).

- richer countries have cut housing, education and health budgets. At least 350,000 households are now homeless in Britain as a result (Shelter, 1995). When housing is in short supply, it is easy to scapegoat an outsider, such as the refugee.

- in richer countries, direct assistance to asylum-seekers and refugees has been cut. For example, in Britain, Section 11 Provision (a funding arrangement from the Local Government Act 1966, used to fund English as an Additional Language (EAL) work in schools) has been cut by 43 per cent since 1992. Welfare benefits for the majority of asylum-seekers were cut in 1996. In many cases lack of support for projects working with newly-arrived asylum-seekers have prevented them successfully integrating into their new communities, forever keeping them as outsiders (Carey-Wood et al, 1995; Refugee Council, 1996a).

While refugee numbers increase, so do the hurdles placed in the way of people who want to flee. Since the mid-1980s it has become increasingly difficult for asylum-seekers to gain entry to EU countries. For those asylum-seekers who have managed to enter, it has become harder than ever to gain refugee status: the vast majority of asylum-seekers are now afforded temporary protection, or are refused. The introduction of these restrictive measures has been mainly caused by an increase in racism, nationalism and xenophobia in Europe but politicians and governments have also contributed to hostility to 'outsiders'. In Britain the pejorative remarks of some Conservative politicians during the passage of the Asylum and Immigration (Appeals) Act 1993 and the Asylum and Immigration Act 1996 are witness to this.

The 1990s have seen an extension of these barriers to the poor countries who receive most asylum seekers. Who can blame them: if the richer countries of the world fail to accept responsibility for refugees, it is unrealistic to expect poor countries to have permanently open borders. In the 1990s, large numbers of Sri Lankan Tamils have been repatriated from India, Burmese Rohingyas have been repatriated from Bangladesh. Ghana and Nigeria have refused asylum to Liberians. Some human rights activists believe that a new international system to protect refugees is needed and the 1951 UN Convention Relating to the Status of Refugees will not survive the millennium.

In the wake of increased numbers of asylum-seekers and increased migration from the poorer and more unstable parts of the world, governments of EU states and transnational institutions such as the European Commission must deal with the critical issue of who needs protection in today's world. How can those fleeing armed conflict be afforded protection? How can those fleeing a generally unstable situation be afforded protection? Policy makers in international bodies, governments and non-governmental organisations must respond to this challenge.

Refugees in Britain

The migration of refugees to Britain is by no means a new trend. In the mid-19th century London was probably the refugee capital of the world, as the city gave sanctuary to large numbers of exiles from Europe. The latter half of the 19th century saw the mass exodus of eastern European Jews, some 350,000 of whom settled in Britain.

Over 250,000 Belgians arrived in Britain in 1914 after the invasion of their country. Most returned immediately after hostilities ceased in 1918. Some 56,000 refugees from Nazi Germany, Austria and Czechoslovakia arrived in Britain between 1933 and 1939. The majority of them were Jewish. They arrived at a time when there was fascist-inspired hostility to refugees and when the international community was unable to agree on an acceptable solution to the flight of refugees from Nazi-occupied Europe. In early 1933 leaders of Britain's Jewish community met with Home Office ministers and agreed to meet all the expenses of Jewish refugees. Voluntary agencies, mostly run by Jewish and Quaker groups, were formed to support the new refugees. Despite public hostility and government indifference, the Jewish refugees of 1933-39 brought immense talent to Britain. Among their numbers were 16 people who became Nobel laureates.

The era of the Second World War brought 4,000 unaccompanied refugee children from the Basque country, escaping the fascist army of General Franco. They were met with public sympathy, largely because they were children.

During and after the Second World War some 250,000 Polish nationals settled in Britain. They arrived in several waves: General Sikorski's army and government-in-exile in 1940, the soldiers and dependants of General Anders' army who arrived in 1945/46, Polish nationals in refugee camps in the British sector of Germany, the 14,000 Poles admitted on the European Volunteer Worker scheme and those who fled the new communist government in Poland. Most of the refugees were settled in hostels and army camps and then organised into the Polish Resettlement Corps. They were then billeted to work in key industries such as mining, construction and agriculture. The arrangements for the resettlement of Polish refugees were given legal status with the passage of the Polish Resettlement Act in 1947. This period

was unique in British history as the Government assumed full responsibility for the reception and resettlement of refugees. The reception of
the Poles was generally well planned.

In 1950 the responsibility for co-ordinating the reception of refugees
was handed to a non-governmental organisation: the British Council
for Aid to Refugees (BCAR) (a predecessor organisation of the British
Refugee Council). This was a small organisation which expanded
rapidly in November 1946 with the arrival of 21,000 Hungarian
refugees. BCAR and the National Coal Board were the two agencies
who arranged for the reception and resettlement of the Hungarians.
The refugees were first accommodated in reception hostels and then
moved to independent housing throughout Britain. The Hungarians
were followed by Czechs and other refugees from Eastern Europe. At
the height of the Cold War there was sympathy for these refugees who
had escaped enemy regimes.

Some 24,000 Vietnamese refugees were admitted to the UK between
1979 and 1992. Unlike most other asylum-seekers of this period, the
Vietnamese were 'programme refugees'. Their status was determined
abroad, mostly in the refugee camps of Hong Kong. After arrival in
Britain they were accommodated in reception centres run by organisation such as the British Refugee Council, Save the Children, Refugee
Action and the Ockenden Venture. They remained there for about three
months before being moved to their own homes. Those who arrived on
the First Vietnamese Programme between 1980 and 1984 were dispersed throughout Britain. Within two years of arriving here many had
moved again: to London, Manchester or Birmingham. The policy of
dispersing refugees was acknowledged to be a mistake. The refugees
who arrived on the Second and Third Vietnamese Programmes were
settled in 'cluster areas' where there was an existing Vietnamese
community.

Today, recently-arrived refugees have mostly fled from African and
Asian countries. Table 2.3 shows the main counties of origin of
asylum-seekers in 1995. Since 1985 some 270,000 people have arrived
in Britain as asylum-seekers and their immediate families, the vast
majority of whom have remained in Greater London (Home Office,
1995). Using local authority language surveys it is estimated that some

Table 2.3 Main countries of origin of refugee children in British schools 1995

Country	Number	Most usual home language
Colombia	525	Spanish
Poland	1210	Polish, Romany[1]
Romania	770	Romanian Romany
Turkey	1820	Turkish and/or Kurdish (Kurmanji)[2]
Former Yugoslavia	1,565	Serbo-Croat/Bosnian, Albanian
Iran	615	Farsi[3]
Iraq	930	Arabic, Kurdish (Sorani)
Algeria	1865	Arabic, French, Kabyle
Angola	555	Portuguese, sometimes Umbundu, Kimbundu, Kikongo
Ethiopia	585	Amharic, Oromo, Tigrinya
Ghana	1915	English, Twi, Fante, Ewe, Ga
Kenya	1395	English, Swahili, Kikuyu, Luo, etc.
Liberia	390	English, Krio, Kpelle
Nigeria	5825	English, Yoruba, Ibo, Fulani, Hausa
Sierra Leone	855	Krio, English, Mende, Temne
Somalia	3465	Somali, Brava, Arabic[4]
Sudan	345	Arabic, Dinka, Nuer and other southern languages, English
Tanzania	1535	Swahili, English
Uganda	365	English, Luganda
Zaire	935	French, Lingala, Kikongo
Afghanistan	580	Dari, Pushtu[5]
China	790	Mandarin Chinese, Cantonese
India	3255	Mostly Punjabi
Pakistan	2915	Urdu
Sri Lanka	2070	Tamil

1   The majority of Polish asylum-seekers in 1995 were Gypsies.

2.   In Turkey it has been forbidden to speak or publish Kurdish until very recently. As a result few families are literate in Kurdish.

3.   The Persian language is usually referred to as Farsi in Iran and Dari in Afghanistan.

4.   Many recent refugees from Somalia are from the Brava community who live in the southern coastal towns. They speak a dialect of Swahili called Brava.

5.   C.f. note 3 above

From Rutter (1997)

88 per cent of Britain's 46,000 school-aged refugee children are living in Greater London (Refugee Council, 1997).

Although there is a great deal of legislation concerning asylum (see Table 2.4), there is no British government policy on the reception and resettlement of asylum-seekers and refugees. The current policy is very much one of 'laissez faire'. Asylum-seekers and refugees may live wherever they want (or can). There are few direct services provided to give them additional support to enable them to resettle. Outside education, most direct services to refugees are provided by non-governmental organisation. Co-ordination between different government departments on refugee resettlement issues is poor. Few local authorities have co-ordinated refugee policies. In this respect Britain differs from EU countries such as the Netherlands and Denmark which have demarcated government strategies and reception facilities.

Refugee children's backgrounds

It is very important for teachers to appreciate the variety of refugee children's backgrounds and prior experiences. Within a particular national group, refugees come from different ethnic, religious and political groups. Refugees' class origins differ, although some generalisations can be made: those who have fled the world's poorest countries are primarily the urban middle classes.

Refugees' educational backgrounds differ too. Among refugee children, some have a fairly complete education in their home country. Other refugee children may have had a much interrupted education in their countries of origin, usually because civil war has closed schools.

Refugee children's experiences of persecution vary widely too, even among nationals from the same country. A few children may never have experienced persecution as their parents may have been resident in Britain when regimes/events at home changed. Other children may have experienced multiple and/or prolonged trauma. There have been many attempts to quantify the traumatic experiences of refugee children, and the results of such studies make illuminating (and shocking) reading for teachers. For example, Mona Maksoud attempted to assess war trauma among Lebanese children (Maksoud, 1992). A representative sample of 2,200 Lebanese children were selected, and parents were asked to report on the potentially traumatic events experienced by their children. The results showed that

- 90.3 per cent of the children had experienced shelling or combat

- 68.4 per cent of the children had been forcibly displaced from home

- 54.5 per cent of the children had experienced grave shortages of food, water and other necessities

- 50.3 per cent of the children had witnessed violent acts such as murder

- 26 per cent of children had lost family and/or friends

- 21.3 per cent of the children had become separated from their families

- 5.9 per cent of the children had been injured

- 3.5 per cent of the children were victims of violent acts such as arrest, detention and torture

- 0.2 per cent of the children were forced to join militias.

In addition, she found that older children, boys and children from poorer families were more likely to have experienced multiple traumatic events. Research carried out by Naomi Richman in the London Borough of Hackney highlights the fact that many refugee children have also experienced a change of carer. In her sample of 33 children some 14 experienced a change of carer. (William Yule discusses the psychological and educational implications of such events in Chapter Five.)

Legislative and policy changes in Britain: the effects on refugee children

As was discussed earlier in this chapter, legislative and policy changes have been enacted throughout Europe targeted at the refugee and asylum-seeker. These changes have had these effects

- barriers such as visas and carriers' sanctions to keep asylum-seekers out of Europe

- reductions in asylum-seekers' social rights within European countries

- a reduction in the proportion of asylum-seekers who are granted refugee status leave to remain in their countries of asylum

- a trend towards the harmonisation of European asylum policy facilitated by the intergovernmental Steering Group on Immigration and Asylum. This group is not accountable to elected bodies such as the European Parliament or individual parliaments, but has formulated treaties and agreements that have a major effect on the lives of individual asylum-seekers.

Table 2.4 details legal changes in British asylum policy. Many of these legal changes present severe obstacles to asylum-seekers who wish to rebuild their lives in Britain. Mental health professionals working with asylum-seekers who have survived severe human rights violations at home are now referring to a process of 'retraumatisation'. This describes the effect of stress in Britain. Retraumatisation occurs because asylum-seekers are being denied access to family reunion, certainty of immigration status, decent housing, welfare benefits and EAL classes. Children, as well as adults, are being retraumatised.

These British legal and policy changes have further multiple and inter-related effects on refugee children. Probably the most important ones are

- the above changes and press coverage associated with legislation such as the Asylum and Immigration (Appeals) Act 1993 and the Asylum and Immigration Act 1996 have contributed to an increase in hostility to refugees, including children in schools

- a tightening of access to permanent, public sector accommodation, as a result of the Asylum and Immigration (Appeals) Act 1993 and the Asylum and Immigration Act 1996 has resulted in an increased mobility among refugee children. It has become more difficult for them to settle into one school and rebuild lives and educational careers

- a reduction in access to benefits means that many asylum-seeking families are living in straitened circumstance

Table 2.4. Legislative and Policy Changes Affecting Asylum-Seekers 1984-1996

1984 Greater proportions of asylum-seekers are awarded ELR rather than refugee status.

1985 Visas requirements are introduced for Sri Lankan nationals, making it more difficult for Tamils fleeing Sri Lanka to reach safety.

1986 Visa requirements introduced for Ghanaians.

1987 Immigration (Carriers' Liability) Act passed. This fines airlines and other carriers, for transporting passengers, often potential asylum-seekers, who lack the correct travel documents. It makes airline employees into surrogate immigration officers.

Social security regulations change with asylum-seekers being reduced to 90 per cent of personal allowances.

1989 Visas introduced for Turkish nationals after Turkish Kurdish asylum-seekers arrive in Britain.

1990 Visas introduced for Ugandans. The Dublin Convention is signed between 12 EU countries. This outlines the country which is responsible for hearing an asylum application, and prevents an asylum-seeker lodging more than one asylum application in the EU.

1992 The 12 EU countries sign the Edinburgh Declaration on 'manifestly unfounded asylum applications' calling for the introduction of swift ejection procedures for those judged to have a 'manifestly unfounded' claim for asylum.

Visas are introduced for Bosnian nationals.

1993 The Asylum and Immigration (Appeals) Act and associated changes in immigration rules. This introduces a 'fast track' system at ports of entry and restricts the rights of asylum-seekers to be housed in permanent local authority accommodation.

The proportions of asylum-seekers who are rejected increases from 16% to 76%.

1994 Visas for Sierra Leonean nationals.

1996 The Asylum and Immigration Act. This cuts welfare benefits for asylum-seekers who apply in-country and those appealing against a negative decision, restricts access to local authority housing, and deems some countries of origin 'safe', *inter alia*.

- the reduction in the proportion of asylum-seekers awarded refugee status and ELR to an all time low means that families are living in great uncertainty. This may be reflected in high levels of stress among asylum-seeking families, including children.

Once in Britain refugee families have varied experiences in finding advice, housing, employment, education and other services. The Home Office and several local authorities have researched refugees' experiences in Britain (Carey-Wood et al., 1995, London Borough of Brent, 1993, Barnet Borough Voluntary Service Council, 1995). The findings of such research indicate that

- resolving asylum applications is the most pressing need of asylum-seekers

- many asylum-seekers lack access to good quality legal advice, particularly for immigration appeals

- housing problems are the second most important issue faced by asylum-seekers

- almost all asylum-seekers spend time in temporary accommodation. This has implications for other services such as health and education

- about 70 per cent of adult asylum-seekers speak little or no English on arrival in Britain

- unemployment rates are high, even among those refugees who have been in Britain for a long period of time

- many adult asylum-seekers have completed higher educational courses at home – refugees are a much better educated group than the population as a whole – and have suffered a major fall in their standard of living in migrating to Britain

Although it is important not to make assumptions when working with refugee children, teachers should be aware of past and current stressors. Newly-arrived refugee children are more likely to

- have parents who speak little English

- be living in temporary accommodation

- have had several moves of school due to changes in accommodation

- be coping with poverty

- have suffered a large drop in their standard of living

In 1989, an opinion poll conducted at the time of deportations of Vietnamese from Hong Kong indicated that some 58 per cent of the British public felt there were too many refugees in Britain. A similar poll was repeated in 1992, at the start of debate around the Asylum and Immigration (Appeals) Bill. This indicated that some 73 per cent of the sample felt there were too many refugees in Britain. Negative media coverage in most tabloid newspapers undoubtedly contributed to this increase in hostility. In parts of London at this time 'bogus' became a playground taunt for refugees.

Little research has been done about children's perceptions of refugees among them, and the author is mostly relying on testimonies and anecdotal evidence. Peer hostility to refugees is something that is reported by many refugee children and young people. Naomi Richman's research in the London Borough of Hackney highlighted the extent of bullying experienced by newly-arrived refugee children. Of her sample of 33 children some 19 reported bullying as a major factor affecting their lives, and seven had had to move school as a result of bullying. Refugee children reported to the author experiences which range from being ignored, to verbal abuse and physical abuse. Some refugee parents have gone as far as removing their children from some London secondary schools, because their children felt so unsafe. A high level of fear is not conducive to effective learning. As one student stated, 'Once I even got beaten up by a group of students who used to bully everyone. They said they couldn't stand me because I was a refugee and lived on the Government's money (which they considered to be their own money). After this I lost all my confidence...'

Among some young people there are differing perceptions of refugees. Some, such as Bosnians, may be considered 'deserving', others, mostly Black Africans, as less so. There is a need for more research into young people's perceptions of refugee students, and how these perceptions are formed. There is also a need to evaluate school measures to counter racist bullying. Negative feelings towards refugees can also affect the level of services offered to support them. At a time of scarce resources, local authorities may be less willing to make funds available to support unpopular groups, particularly those that do not have a vote. This again impacts on children.

Almost all asylum-seeking families have relied on the provision of social housing when they first arrive in Britain. Until 1993, this was provided, guided by the Housing Act 1985. For most families, this meant a period of time in temporary accommodation before somewhere more settled was found. (An estimated 8,000-10,000 asylum-seeking children are living in temporary accommodation In Greater London (Refugee Council, 1996a)) Three pieces of legislation have now sought to restrict asylum-seekers rights to social housing. Since 1993, a greater number of asylum-seeking children have been housed in temporary accommodation, for a greater period of time. And since 1993, a greater number of asylum-seeking children have been accommodated in private sector housing. The effects of housing legislation on the education of asylum-seeking and refugee children are discussed in more detail in Chapter Three.

As well as restricting access to social housing, the Asylum and Immigration Act 1996 also restricts asylum-seekers access to welfare benefits. Asylum-seekers who apply 'in-country' (some 65 per cent of all asylum-seekers) and those appealing against a negative decision are not entitled to any welfare benefits, including income support, child benefit, housing benefit, free school meals and other provisions afforded to families claiming income support. In most cases those without access to benefits have been left destitute. The Refugee Council estimates that some 8,000 children will be affected by the withdrawal of benefits by the end of 1996 (Refugee Council, 1996a).

Local authorities have been left to pick up the pieces, under the provisions of the Children Act 1989. Under Section 17 of this Act, local authorities are obliged to provide services to 'safeguard and promote the welfare of children in need'. By mid April, 1997, London social services departments have been obliged to provide subsistence allowances and housing to some 2,375 families affected by the withdrawal of benefits, mostly without any extra funding from central government. This will lead to cuts in other non-statutory services. At the time of writing many social services departments were voicing disquiet that they had become an 'alternative Department of Social Security'. Even those families who still have benefits are being affected. Most single asylum-seekers denied benefits have become reliant on other members of their own community to support them. Some refugee families are sharing their already meagre resources among more and more people.

Schools and other agencies are already noticing the ill effects of the withdrawal of such benefits. Some children have simply disappeared from roll. It is likely that among asylum-seeking children there will be

- an increase in malnutrition and associated health problems

- the manifestation of stress-related illness among affected children

- greater family breakdown

- little effective learning in schools.

In the long term the costs to society of the withdrawal of benefits may be greater than any money saved. It is hoped that the new government, elected while this book was being edited, will reinstate benefits to asylum-seekers.

Future trends

The next five years are likely to see further changes for the world's refugees and asylum-seekers. Although it is very difficult to make accurate predictions, the following challenges may face the world's refugees and those who work with them.

- More closed borders and greater numbers of forced repatriations, further weakening the 1951 UN Convention Relating to the Status of Refugees.

- A downgrading in UNHCR's role in legal protection as a result of pressure from western governments, its major funder

- A greater reliance on temporary protection for those fleeing persecution and conflict. This situation has already been rehearsed for those fleeing the conflict in former Yugoslavia. A good number were only granted temporary status in the countries to which they fled. (The greater reliance on temporary protection has educational implications: if children are to remain in a country of asylum for a short period of time, how should they be educated?)

• A greater involvement of European Union institutions in the determination of asylum and refugee settlement policy in Britain as part of the trend towards harmonising European asylum and immigration policy. In February 1996 the EU Council of Ministers produced a draft memorandum on the minimum reception conditions for asylum-seekers. This was the first time that the EU had pronounced on the social conditions of asylum-seekers. European asylum policy will also be brought within the competence of European Commission and European Parliament, rather than being decided in the non-accountable Steering Group on Immigration and Asylum (an intergovernmental group) as today

• Within Europe a larger number of asylum-seekers 'going underground' after being refused asylum, and perhaps the deliberate targeting of those who lack legal immigration status, and those who work to support them. Already some EU countries penalise non-governmental organisations who work with undocumented immigrants, including children

• A major review of British asylum and settlement policy. Asylum procedures may be shortened and some asylum-seekers may be accommodated in reception centres. Asylum-seekers may again be dispersed throughout Britain (On 15th May, 1997, the London Borough of Westminster announced that it was to move some 125 asylum-seekers from hostels in the capital to a hostel in Liverpool). It is very likely that a greater proportion of those who have failed to gain asylum will be removed or deported.

Those involved in the education of refugee children must be prepared for these changes. Teachers and educationalists must consider the long term aims of education for children who may only be in the UK for a limited period. We must consider effective ways of supporting children, whatever their legal status. We must consider the educational implications of settling children in reception centres and of a government policy to settle them throughout the UK. For these reasons the provision of an appropriate education for refugee children will remain a pressing and complex issue for many years to come.

CHAPTER THREE

Refugees, Asylum Seekers and the Housing Crisis: No Place to Learn

Sally Power, Geoff Whitty and Deborah Youdell

Introduction

Strategies designed to improve the educational opportunities of asylum-seekers and refugees are unlikely to succeed unless they take account of the broader public policy context. In particular, educators need to be aware of the inadequate and uncertain housing situation of many asylum-seekers and refugees. When they are already attempting to deal with the trauma of their dislocation and intimidating bureau-cratic procedures, homelessness confronts asylum-seekers with an additional set of problems.

This chapter looks at ways in which homelessness impedes access to appropriate educational provision. It is based on research funded by Shelter and draws on a range of data, including a national survey of local education authorities (LEAs), in-depth research with education professionals at local government and school level in three areas of the country, and personal accounts of homeless parents and children – some of whom were asylum-seekers or refugees (for further details see Power et al, 1995).

The first section outlines the key aspects of housing policy and practice as it relates to asylum-seekers in the current homelessness crisis. The second section looks at the difficulties that homeless families face in trying to obtain educational provision, while the third section explores some of the ways in which living in inadequate and uncertain accommodation hinders the educational progress of homeless children in general and asylum-seekers and refugees in particular. The fourth section looks at the role of the school as a refuge and barriers to effective support. Finally, we outline a number of recommendations which may help prevent schools adding further obstacles to the already disrupted educational careers of refugee and asylum-seeking children.

Asylum-seekers, refugees and the housing crisis

In a country in which homelessness is a chronic and escalating problem, it is perhaps not surprising that asylum-seekers and refugees are regularly assigned accommodation that is temporary and inadequate. They represent only one small element of the 350,000 who currently apply to housing departments every year (Butler et al, 1994) with the hope of being accommodated from an ever-dwindling supply of social housing.

Refugees and homelessness

The legal status of those who have fled to Britain affects their entitlement to housing. Families, with full refugee status or Exceptional Leave to Remain (ELR) follow the same procedures as other groups of homeless persons. In order to be eligible for assistance in securing accommodation, households need to be defined as 'statutorily homeless'. This means that they must be homeless (or threatened with imminent homelessness), not intentionally homeless; in 'priority need', which includes households with dependent children, and holding a connection with that local authority (for a refugee this usually means their first point of contact). Once an applicant is accepted as fulfilling these criteria, the local authority is obliged to secure accommodation for them and their cohabitants, even if this is of a temporary nature.

The nature of interim housing measures varies from local authority to local authority, but they usually involve a combination of short-term private sector leased (PSL) accommodation, hostels and bed and breakfast hotels. Although there are problems with all these forms of accommodation, the bed and breakfast hotel is most notorious. As a result of concerted campaigns, escalating costs and administrative difficulties, some local authorities, such as Camden and Leicester, have stopped using bed and breakfast accommodation altogether. However, local authority initiatives are being overtaken by central government policies designed to augment the role of the private sector in providing temporary housing. This may well lead us back to an increased use of bed and breakfast hotels and other forms of substandard and un-regulated accommodation.

The current obligation on authorities to find accommodation for homeless households is not framed within any time limit. Jencks (1994), commenting on a similar situation in the United States argues that the term 'temporary' is as much a political expedient as an accurate description. 'The government cannot put families in one room indefinitely without becoming embroiled in political and legal controversies that most politicians desperately want to avoid. So when the government puts families in a single room, everybody has an interest in claiming the situation is only temporary'. In this country the average length of stay in temporary accommodation is three months (Shelter, 1994), but some families remain in such housing for many years. Sharma's survey of one hundred families living in bed and breakfast accommodation in Hounslow revealed that one quarter of the sample had been there for more than one year and were likely to end up staying there much longer. Similarly, users of the Bayswater Hotel Homeless Project talk of being in bed and breakfast accommodation for up to two years (Crane, 1990). One refugee family in our research is now in its third year of being moved from bed and breakfast hotels to private short-term leases and then back to bed and breakfast.

The future obligation placed on local authorities to secure any form of accommodation has been weakened by the Housing Act 1996. The Housing Act contains a number of measures which diminish the housing prospects of the homeless. It will repeal existing legislation concerning the rights of homeless persons. Even officially 'homeless' households will no longer receive priority on the local authority waiting lists for permanent homes. In addition, local authorities will have the discretion to turn away homeless families, even with young children, simply on the basis that accommodation is available in the area.

Asylum-seekers and homelessness

Asylum-seekers face additional problems in securing homes. They are disadvantaged through government policy which appears to be based on the premise that they will 'jump' the housing queue – reflecting and reinforcing media myths of 'floods' of immigrants 'scrounging off the British welfare system. (e.g. Williams, 1996).

Thus, the Asylum and Immigration (Appeals) Act 1993 applies stricter rules to homeless asylum-seekers than any other category of homeless people. For instance, asylum-seekers cannot be accepted as homeless if they have access to any available accommodation, 'however temporary'. Staying with relatives or friends for just one night renders them ineligible, acting as a disincentive for others to help out. Moreover while the immigration status of the asylum-seeker is being considered, the housing authority cannot make any offer of a secure social housing tenancy. As asylum applications often take a long time to process, families may spend extended periods in temporary accommodation – spells that are further extended when an asylum-seeker is given a decision on their case. Many asylum-seekers are now placing themselves in bed and breakfast hotels (Carter, 1995).

The Housing Act 1996 and the Asylum and Immigration Act 1996 exclude asylum-seekers from access to housing waiting list, worsening an already bad situation. The Asylum and Immigration Act 1996 also deprives two groups of asylum-seekers of access to benefits. (Those who apply in-country and those appealing against a negative decision are now deprived of access to benefits). Families with children are now being housed by local authorities under the provisions of the Children Act 1989 in accommodation of a very temporary nature.

In summary, the housing situation faced by asylum-seekers is bleak – and set to worsen. Along with many other tens of thousands of households, they find themselves trapped in temporary accommodation with little knowledge of how long they are likely to remain there. However, such children still have full rights to educational provision. But, while it is clear that schools might provide a secure environment for these dislocated children, the uncertain and inadequate nature of their accommodation often makes them unable to take advantage of their educational entitlement.

No home – no school

Difficulties securing accommodation translate into difficulties securing education. It is impossible to gauge the overall number of children who are out of school at any one time, but it is clear from our research and that of others that many homeless children fall through the educational safety net. High rates of non-attendance have led some to claim that schooling is not important to homeless families. In our research a few LEA staff suggested that children were kept out of school intentionally, for example ... a lot of parents use homelessness as an excuse for not pushing their children...' However, a rather different picture was painted by families themselves. School was seen to provide security and a sense of normality for a child whose life was otherwise extremely unsettled. In fact, the constraints of temporary accommodation meant that not sending the children to school could put a tremendous strain on family relationships. As one mother put it 'I'm desperate to get them into school. It's doing my head in'. The father of a family of refugees who had been placed in a bed and breakfast hotel commented:

> Having children out of school is very difficult. They are always complaining that they are out of school. It is difficult to contain them in this space all day. They children blame me that they are out of school.

Difficulties securing a school place can be accounted for in a variety of ways – shortage of supply, the poor 'market position' of homeless families and an inadequate supply of information.

School places become in short supply when schools are oversubscribed as a result of either their location in neighbourhoods with high population densities and/or of their popularity with parents. The former is a particular problem in areas where there a high concentration of hotels used by homeless families. In parts of inner London this shortage is acute. An HMI report notes that parents had difficulties in finding places in Camden and Westminster, at nursery and reception as well as on transfer to secondary school (HMI, 1990). In one of our case study areas, two thirds of the school had no places available. In another, the problem was not borough-wide, but affected two schools serving the hostels for the homeless. In both areas, the effect was the same: 'I went around all of the schools, they said they were full. I filled in application forms, now we are on the waiting list'.

Large families that we spoke to found it particularly difficult to find places for all their children in a single school. One family, Eritrean asylum-seekers, was only able to find a school place for one of the six children. Two had been promised places within the next few months, but the other three children, aged 12, ten and eight years, had to be placed on a waiting list with little indication of when a space might be available. Children of refugees and asylum-seekers, in particular, appear to suffer from delays in registering with a new school (Murie and Jeffers, 1987, Sharma, 1987).

One of the reasons why these groups have difficulty getting a school place is related to their poor market position. Recent education policy may result in schools being increasingly less able or willing to take homeless pupils, particularly those from refugee or asylum seeking families. The policy of open enrolment means that places are no longer protected for children within a catchment area. Moreover, the move towards education markets through the publication of performance indicators has made some pupils seem more of a liability than others. Refugee children, together with other homeless children, may be poor achievers and attenders for a variety of reasons. And while we have no direct evidence of schools refusing places to children living in temporary accommodation on these grounds, there is certainly suspicion among some local government officers that certain schools were discriminatory in their enrolment practices.

An additional obstacle in obtaining a school place undoubtedly relates to inadequate information, both for parents and professionals. Homeless households, especially in London, are often placed in accommodation in a borough about which they have little local knowledge. This can be major obstacle for families who are new to the UK, especially if English is not their first language. Indeed, refugees and asylum-seekers are likely to be unfamiliar not only with the particular area, but with the English education system as a whole. Furthermore, cuts in budgets held by LEAs make it increasingly difficult for the Education Welfare Services to target homeless families. And while we spoke with some local government officers and voluntary sector workers who would go to hostels and bed and breakfast hotels to assist families find school places, this was not possible where households were dispersed into short-let private sector accommodation. – as is increasingly the case. In short, the provision of relevant advice and guidance was generally considered to be largely a matter of 'luck'.

Our survey of English LEAs revealed that very few received regular information from housing officers about the placement of homeless families. Although there was often informal liaison, this tended to be ad hoc. For instance, one education officer said that such notification had been requested on a number of occasions but that 'the response to this is somewhat haphazard depending on the importance placed on this request by an individual worker.' A major concern must be the complete lack of communication from housing authorities placing families in temporary accommodation outside their boundaries. Where this was the case, liaison was unknown. The existence and whereabouts of asylum-seekers forced to place *themselves* in temporary accommodation is unknown even to housing officers.

Temporary Accommodation and Pupil Progress

An unsatisfactory housing situation can create a range of problems for the refugee child, even after he or she has secured a place at school. Our research, like that of others, identifies a number of ways in which living in temporary accommodation impacts negatively on the educational experiences and opportunities of the homeless child. These can be broadly classified into factors associated with the conditions and location of accommodation, its uncertain and temporary nature, and the social stigma of homelessness.

Poor housing conditions

The nature of emergency housing varies. Bed and breakfast hotels are probably the most damaging, as we have seen, they are increasingly used by asylum-seekers who have no other option. As already mentioned, this 'emergency housing' can be anything but short term. Families are often forced to endure cramped and squalid conditions for months, even years.

A range of studies has shown that poor housing in general, and temporary accommodation in particular, has adverse consequences for the physical and psychosocial development of children. For instance the Black Report (DHSS, 1980) established a causal relationship between the type of housing tenure and poor health. Seven years later, the National Children's Bureau (1987) provided further evidence that poor housing and homelessness were detrimental to child health. Other research and surveys reveal that living in temporary accommodation, particularly in bed and breakfast hotels, had negative health aspects which are likely to be anything but temporary (Howarth, 1987, Morton, 1988). Furley (1989) cites evidence that overcrowded hotel accommodation results in high accident rates. The father of one family of asylum-seekers were visited had recently sustained a severe and permanently disabling injury when trying to open the bedroom window for ventilation. Children were constantly at risk of scalding as they accompanied parents returning from the basement kitchen with pans of hot food and liquid.

In addition to ill-health, poor housing adversely affects other aspects of a child's development. Overcrowding has been shown to result in a range of problems. For young children, the limitations of bed and breakfast and lack of play space can be particularly restrictive (Edwards, 1992). Lack of facilities for play is often compounded by the fear of racial abuse and harassment experienced by many black and ethnic minority families living in such accommodation. Such fears may force children and parents to remain in their own rooms even where facilities exist (e.g. Sharma, 1987, Muries and Jeffers, 1987).

Cramped and confined conditions have been shown to lead to socio-economic difficulties. Children of families we visited often appeared silent, withdrawn and lethargic. One family of eight Somali refugees who had spent the last three years in temporary accommodation were now living in one room of a bed and breakfast hotel. Again, not all the children could get into schools. The six year old boy occupied his days by sleeping. Other parents had observed how their children's behaviour had changed. One mother whose children had been out of school for ten weeks said:

..it's really bad for them and us.. in the time we've been here they are changed kids, they have nothing to occupy their brains...they are all getting on top of each other, it's hard to occupy them, they are getting into mischief and my patience is wearing thin.

Similarly, one father reported that his son's behaviour had been adversely affected by living in a bed and breakfast hotel:

he shows off, he's hyperactive, he's been in trouble with the head teacher... he sleeps better when he's at school because it tires him out and it doesn't help being stuck here in one room all the time.

For older children, the problem with such accommodation is not lack of play space but lack of study space. The cramped conditions create problems in completing homework and course projects out of school hours. Again, bed and breakfast accommodation was widely felt to cause the greatest damage to pupils' academic performance, for example '... the children don't seem to be able to concentrate on their homework in this single room..' '...the children take it in turns to do their homework at the table'. Great effort is needed to keep up with school work in these conditions. 'When we are off school, I try to get my work done. I try to do extra things I am not good at. I try to work, to keep up... we just go to the library.' One head teacher reported that homework assignments given to pupils living in bed and breakfast accommodation were modified to ensure that they were achievable. However, providing less challenging work for these pupils may well contribute to underachievement in the longer term.

Lack of facilities in temporary accommodation also hampered home-school contacts. Over half of head teachers whose schools had home-less pupils reported problems in maintaining contact with parents of pupils living in temporary accommodation. A number of schools claimed that they were not always informed of changes of address when families were forced to move on. Difficulties with contact were most often mentioned in connection with bed and breakfast hotels and hostels. Teachers could not reach parents and there were insufficient phones for parents to call schools. However, it is hard to imagine that the situation will be much improved with the increasing use of private sector accommodation. Indeed it may be worsened. Few families will have their own phones, or even access to a shared one.

The uncertainty of temporary accommodation

Uncertainty is another key feature of living in temporary accommodation that prevents homeless children getting the educational opportunities they so badly need. Although homeless families may be placed in temporary accommodation for extended periods, they are never sure how long they will remain in one place or when they will be moved to the next. The families in our survey spoke of being moved at short notice and not being kept informed by housing officers about how long they were likely to spend in their next location. For asylum-seekers this uncertainty has an added dimension as they await news not just of their future homes but of their continued residency in the country. Not surprisingly, this disruption and uncertainty leads to feelings of insecurity, dilemmas over children's education, frequent changes in schools and associated problems with educational continuity and integration.

Never knowing how long one is going to stay in any one place presents families with a number of dilemmas when considering what to do about education. Parents are often understandably reluctant to move their children each time they change address. Black and other minority ethnic parents in particular may be unwilling to send their children to new schools because of fear of racial abuse and harassment (Murie and Jeffers, 1987, ILEA, 1987). In some cases schools in the new area are not appropriate for and/or have insufficient experience to deal with bilingual students (Sharma, 1987).

As a result, many parents and children make great sacrifices to travel substantial distances. Students often arrive at school late without having eaten breakfast. Sometimes this is because of inadequate cooking facilities in hotels and hostels, sometimes it stems from the long journeys that children have to make before they reach school. Where the family has been moved and the children are kept at their 'old' schools costs of transport could be incurred. One family of asylum-seekers from the Gulf was having to find £6.40 every day out of its income support to transport the children to school. Only one of the families in the survey had applied for any help with travel expenses. But then not one of our case study LEAs had any form of guidance specifically related to transport support for families living in temporary accommodation. Even Education Welfare Officers were unclear as to who was responsible for such support or whether a budget was available. Usual criteria for eligibility are designed to cater for the needs of a stable school population which is permanently housed. In addition, diminishing local government resources have meant less money for discretionary help. As one deputy head noted: '...as time as gone on there is less and less money to give that kind of support.'

It is clear that in may cases there is no other alternative than for parents to move their children when they move address – often several times over. The consequences for this for the child's education are all too obvious. The importance of academic continuity for pupil progress and achievement was stressed by teachers at both primary and secondary level: 'The disruption to the continuity of their education leaves gaps in their learning and, no matter how intelligent, it is difficult for them to catch up.'

Frequent moves also hinder homeless pupils' ability to build social relationships within school. As well as trying to pick up their school work again, learning the school layout, timetable and teachers names, students have to build new sets of relationships. Sometimes it can all seem a bit too much. Withdrawal was common among homeless pupils and deliberately not making friends appeared to be strategy adopted by many: 'I don't rush into making friends, I try to get to know people... I'm not keeping my distance, but I'm not making a best friend either.' Similarly another pupils said: 'I'm not worried about other children, I just don't want to talk to them.' One ex-pupil said of her primary and early secondary school career:' Half the time I didn't bother to try and mix because we would only get moved again'.

But problems with settling in are not always to do with reluctance on the part of the homeless pupil – they often arise from the isolation created through the stigma of homelessness itself.

The stigma of homelessness

There are a number of reasons why homeless children are stigmatised. Many are connected with poverty, but are exacerbated by poor housing conditions or frequent moves. For instance, one mother spoke of the frustration of not being able to send her children off to school looking tidy: '...the children's clothes are all screwed up. I can't iron them ... the room is already filled up with suitcases'. Parents also mentioned the problem of affording the uniform each time a child moved school.

However, we should be careful not to explain the stigmatisation of homeless children solely in terms of their personal problems. There is plenty of evidence to suggest that these children suffer as much from the negative social perceptions of homelessness as from the material difficulties which it creates. For many refugees and asylum seekers this exclusion is compounded by racism and xenophobia within the school.

The common perception that homelessness is a sign of personal failure appears to make it hard for children living in temporary accommodation to settle in at school. They can try to hide their homelessness. This causes problems reciprocating friendship. Nearly two thirds of head teachers reported that homelessness had an impact upon relationships with other pupils.

Homeless pupils were generally seen to be 'outsiders.' One mother retold how her son was '...called all sorts of names because he didn't have house'. The problem of bullying was mentioned by several homeless pupils as something to be endured, for example, 'You sometimes get bullied, the teachers can't stop it, they can't help every kid in the school.'

The school as refuge?
Schools are well placed to provide a secure and safe environment for children whose prospects are otherwise bleak. They also provide longer term opportunities which these children badly need if they are to break out of the cycle of disadvantage associated with homelessness. However, while some children did find school a welcome refuge, our research suggests that the educational needs of many homeless students were often unfulfilled. In part, this can be related to inflexibility and lack of awareness on the part of school. But it is also exacerbated by the strain which high numbers of homeless children can place on a school – pressures that look set to be compounded by recent education policies.

Schools are organised with the needs of a stable population in mind and are often unable to meet the needs of pupils whose home circumstances make regular and punctual attendance an impossibility. As HMI (1990) pointed out of homeless pupils: 'When these children meet a school system with opportunities and routines which rely on regular and consistent attendance, sustainable achievement is often beyond their reach'. It is unlikely that schools could ever enable students to recover periods out of school or compensate for the dislocation experienced with every change of school, but some students felt that teachers were sometimes unsympathetic to their circumstances. For instance, schools seemed unaware of the difficulties which homeless students experienced in trying to take part in extra-curricular activities. These can be important in helping children feel that they belong and must have added significance for children whose home life can be so restricted. Yet several pupils spoke of how they had missed out, for example 'I was in the swimming and hockey teams, I missed practices so I got kicked off the teams.'

One reason why schools find it difficult to accommodate the needs of homeless pupils is related to the additional administrative difficulties that their presence creates. In some schools with significant numbers of homeless children, there were high rates of turnover with pupils arriving and leaving frequently. For example one school reported that one third of its population was constantly shifting leading to a turnover of 48 per cent in the previous year. '...two thirds stable, here all the time, then you've got a floating third going round, and round and round.'

This creates a tremendous strain on schools. Almost 60 per cent of head teachers whose schools had homeless pupils on roll reported additional administration – much of this administration is related to pupils' entering and leaving the school. 'It's incredibly time consuming because when children are admitted the secretary not only does the admission but has forms for emergency contacts, forms for permission to go on outings, each child gets a school brochure which cost us £2 to produce, there is liaison with the senior lunch-time supervisor over diet, and chasing up records from the previous school and make sure they come in.'

It is not only rates of chhange associated with homeless that creates administrative difficulties, it is also the timing. Enrolment required the admission of homeless pupils at 'non-standard times' during the school year. School funding formulae are largely calculated on the basis of a static school population and take insufficient account of the peaks and troughs in pupil numbers. A low pupil count at the time of calculation means a shortfall in the budget. One head teacher reported:

> 'When starting back after the summer holidays, 14 children who should have been here were not; we filled in form S22 that week. The numbers were low so we had £22,000 taken out of our budget because of the children I had lost. Within three weeks my number was up again.'

The extra work associated with having high numbers of homeless pupils also appears to have adverse effects on teaching and learning. Over half of the head teachers reported that homelessness had an impact upon classroom management. It created extra work and unstable classes. Schools were compelled to make a range of changes to the ways in which classes were organised in order to accommodate the sudden influxes.

It is possible that the introduction of the National Curriculum has reduced some of the disruption. Within its predefined structure and uniform assessment procedures it is seen by some teachers as a potential framework through which to provide continuity for pupils who experience frequent school moves. '...wherever they have been they have done the National Curriculum for their year group'. However, other teachers felt that the formal requirements got in the way of providing individual help. 'The National Curriculum demands are eroding pastoral support and reducing the energy levels of staff so that spontaneous support is being eroded.'

Two thirds of head teachers reported the strain placed on pastoral provision. Alongside problems of record keeping, this was the most frequently mentioned effect of having homeless pupils in the school. Teachers spoke of 'keeping an eye on them' being 'sensitive to their needs' and 'watching out for stress and being aware of the situation.' Schools with a large number of homeless children felt particularly under-resourced in this area. However, the pressure cannot be measured in resources alone. Several teachers spoke of the emotional costs of becoming closely involved in the pastoral care of homeless pupils only to have them move on again.

In short, while it is clear that schools can, and often do, offer homeless students a refuge from unsatisfactory housing, the organisation of the school and the turbulence of transient populations limits the ability of schools to meet longer term educational objectives. As mentioned earlier, recent educational policies will do little to ease the burden.

The local management of schools (LMS) policy, together with the introduction of grant-maintained schools, has shifted responsibilities and finance away from LEAs to individual schools. This is likely to have implications for the provision of education to homeless children. It certainly means that LEAs are worse placed to plan systematic support across schools and they are likely to have fewer resources to monitor the incidence and impact of homelessness or mitigate its effects.

Recommendations

Clearly it is beyond the scope of educationalists to change immigration or housing policy. Nevertheless there are a number of ways in which we think schools and LEAs can prevent the compounding of educational difficulties faced by homeless asylum-seekers.

At LEA Level. LEAs should monitor the overall incidence and distribution of children living in temporary accommodation attending or requiring admission to schools. This will enable them to target resources and services more effectively.

All LEAs should identify an officer as having key responsibility for the education of homeless children. This will facilitate liaison between different local authority departments and agencies in securing appropriate provision.

A factor specifically related to homelessness should be included in the additional educational needs element of LMS formulae in addition to any allowance already given for overall levels of social disadvantage.

This should be sensitive to fluctuations in pupil numbers and high pupil turnover during the course of the year.

The criteria determining eligibility to and application procedures for financial support such as transport, school uniforms and free school meals should take into account the specific circumstances of homeless families.

Schools and LEAs should devise strategies to facilitate the efficient transfer of records. Prompt receipt of these is essential for the pupil and to minimise administration time.

At School Level Given the difficulties which homeless pupils often face in achieving regular attendance, schools should provide them with flexible learning opportunities. This may involve teachers providing work for pupils to undertake outside school. Schools should also ensure that there are facilities such as homework clubs where homeless pupils can work outside normal lesson time.

In order to minimise the isolation and stigmatisation experienced by homeless pupils, schools should consider the introduction of befriending schemes and other measures to ensure that such children are actively involved in the life of the school.

In order to heighten awareness and understanding, and to provide a more welcoming environment, schools should cover issues relating to refugees and homelessness in the school curriculum.

To conclude, the insecurity of being placed in temporary accommodation adds further disruption at a time when families need support. This is especially true of refugees and asylum-seekers. For children of these families, the added disruption of homelessness can be particularly confusing and distressing. As we have seen, it often means losing the security and stability of school as well as home. Unless positive action is taken to ensure that these children are given genuinely equal educational opportunities, a disrupted home life will continue to lead to a disrupted and disadvantaged school career.

The authors wish to acknowledge the assistance of Krishna Maharaj, HERU, Policy Studies, Institute of Education and Mona Segal, Policy Officer, Shelter.

CHAPTER FOUR

Unaccompanied – but not Unsupported

Louise Williamson

Introduction

As was stated in Chapter Two, the majority of the world's refugees are women and children, at least half the total being children. It is less well-known that some of these are unaccompanied refugee children – without an adult to care for and support them.

So who are these children and what are their circumstances? How can teachers understand a pupil in their class if they are unaware that the young person has come to this country alone and is being looked after by a 19 year old brother? Or that she is the only survivor of a massacre by rebel forces? Or that she thinks her parents must have wanted to get rid of her? Or that she spent nine months in prison after being a child soldier or politically active? Or that she does not want to move from a children's home to foster carers?

It is clear that the term 'unaccompanied refugee children' encompasses many different realities – and just which one may take some time to discover. It is helpful to consider the phenomenon of unaccompanied refugee children world-wide, their settlement in Britain over the last sixty years and who the children are who are arriving unaccompanied today. It is necessary to have an understanding of how their situation is dealt with in international law – the 1951 UN Convention and 1967 Protocol Relating to the Status of Refugees, the 1989 UN Convention on the Rights of the Child and agreements on inter-country adoption and the adoption of refugee children – as well as in domestic law –

notably in the Asylum and Immigration (Appeals) Act 1993, the Children Act 1989 and the Asylum and Immigration Act 1996. This provides the broad framework within which a multi-agency framework for good practice in the support of unaccompanied refugee children and young people can be developed.

Who are unaccompanied refugee children?

The term 'unaccompanied refugee child' carries the following definitions: 'unaccompanied' is taken to mean '...those who are separated from both parents and are not being cared for by an adult who, by law or custom, has responsibility to do so' (United Nations High Commissioner for Refugees [UNHCR] 1994, p 121). According to Article 1 of the United Nations Convention on the Rights of the Child (adopted by the UN General Assembly on 20 November 1989 and came into force on 2 September 1990), a *'child'* is '...every human being below the age of eighteen years unless, under the law applicable to the child, majority is attained earlier.' Finally, the term *'refugee'* is taken to include asylum-seeking children as well as those children whose asylum claims have been determined.

Although the proportion of unaccompanied refugee children and young people may be relatively small – estimated at between three to five per cent of the total number of refugees (Williamson and Moser, 1987) – the numbers may not be. For example, more than 3,500 unaccompanied children were provided with special services in Thailand in 1980-1982 during the influx of refugees from Cambodia (Ressler, Boothby and Steinbock, 1988). Unaccompanied children from Sudan in the 1980s and 1990s, and in Rwanda in the 1990s have also numbered thousands.

The circumstances which lead to there being unaccompanied refugee children vary. In some countries, children as well as adults may be the subjects of political repression in the form of arbitrary arrest, detention and torture. There are all too many distressing accounts of politically motivated maltreatment of children in Amnesty International Yearbooks and other sources (cf. Boyden and Hudson, 1985). As a result, children and young people may need to escape to safety. Elsewhere, it is very easy during war-induced flight for children to be separated from their parents, either by accident or because their parents die. Parents may send their children abroad in order to avoid them facing dangerous fighting or unrest, compulsory military conscription or being abducted in order to become prostitutes for the army. In other cases, parents may take their child to a country of asylum and then return to their country of origin. There have also been instances where children have been removed by aid workers, particularly if it seems likely that the whole family or village has been destroyed.

What is clear is that the majority of the world's unaccompanied refugee children try to move to safety close to home – either in their own country or in a neighbouring state. This is by preference as much as by economic necessity. It is only a very small proportion whose parents, relatives or other sponsors are able to afford to send them further afield, for example, to countries in Europe or North America.

Sometimes people find it hard to understand how parents could send their children such a long way away, all alone – especially the younger ones. However, although this might not prove to be the best option in the long run, there can be no doubt that such hard decisions are made with love, and in what is thought to be in children's best interests. It is a very natural response to want to protect children from harm, albeit by drastic measures – as demonstrated by accounts of the British Government's World War Two evacuation of children overseas (Fethney, 1990) or inland (Wicks, 1989).

The settlement of unaccompanied refugee children in Britain

Although people may be aware that some unaccompanied refugee children make their way to the United Kingdom, few realise that this is no new phenomenon. In response to various political upheavals and disasters this century, many thousands of unaccompanied refugee children have been resettled in Britain. During the Spanish Civil War, nearly 4,000 mainly Basque children – probably the largest contingent of refugee children ever to arrive here in one group – arrived in Southampton in 1937 (Bell, 1996). The flight from Nazi-occupied Europe included unaccompanied refugee children. Louise London provides evidence that in late 1938 and 1939, 'no limit was placed on the numbers of children under 16 who could enter, provided their maintenance was guaranteed', thereby facilitating the arrival of about 10,000 unaccompanied children – almost exclusively Jewish – from Germany and German-occupied territories during that period. This amounted to roughly 13 per cent of the total number of refugees then in Britain.

After the Second World War, unaccompanied children continued to arrive in Britain. At least 466 Hungarian children arrived in 1956 and 1957 following the Hungarian Revolt; between the years 1952 and 1984 the Ockenden Venture, Save the Children and Pestalozzi had cared for approximately 1,000 unaccompanied children, in addition to the Hungarian children already mentioned (British Refugee Council et al, 1984). Between 1979 and spring 1984, up to 300 Vietnamese un-accompanied children had come to Britain either as part of groups rescued at sea by British ships or as members of special programmes (Mougne, 1985). Since then, a small number of unaccompanied children have come from Southeast Asia as part of subsequent government programmes.

In recent years, very few arrivals of unaccompanied children have been planned and agreed on in advance either with the knowledge of the Home Office or a United Kingdom-registered child care agency. Small numbers have arrived with convoys of refugees brought to the United Kingdom by well-wishers, most notably from the former Yugoslavia. Many more children arrive quite independently of any organised scheme and then apply for asylum either at the port of entry or after they have entered the country.

During the late 1980s, it was estimated that around 50-70 un-accompanied children and young people applied for asylum in this way every year (Jockenhövel-Schieke, 1990). The actual numbers may well have been higher because there was no systematic collation of statistics. Then in August and September 1990, a sudden influx of about 180 children – mainly from Eritrea – entered the country (Finlay, 1990). Possibly as a result of this sharp increase, the Immigration Service (Ports) began to record the total number of asylum-seeking children under 16 years of age whom they identified as being unaccompanied at ports of entry – 128 in 1991.* In subsequent years,

Table 4.1: Unaccompanied children referred to Refugee Council Panel of Advisers – breakdown by age and gender

Age in years	April 1994-March 1995			April 1995-March 1996		
	Total	F by age	M	Total	F by age	M
3	0	0	0	1	0	1
4	0	0	0	2	2	0
5	0	0	0	1	1	0
6	0	0	0	3	2	1
7	0	0	0	2	0	2
8	2	1	1	3	1	2
9	4	3	1	8	2	6
10	6	1	5	10	4	6
11	8	3	5	7	1	6
12	12	6	6	12	5	7
13	14	7	7	18	5	13
14	41	21	20	45	15	30
15	83	34	49	81	30	51
16	86	29	57	108	23	85
17	90	30	60	143	33	110
18	6	3	3	12	6	6
19	4	1	3	1	1	0
20	1	1	0	0	0	0
not known	4	3	1	5	2	3
Total by gender: –		143	218		133	328
Total:	361			461		

Table 4.2: Unaccompanied children referred to Refugee Council Panel of Advisers – breakdown by countries of origin

	April 1994-March 1995	April 1995-Dec 1996
Afghanistan	14	25
Albania	15	10
Algeria	5	4
Angola	20	29
Bosnia	2	4
Burundi	0	6
China	10	15
Columbia	1	3
Eritrea	52	44
Ethiopia	73	48
Ghana	8	8
Gambia	0	13
Iran	1	2
Iraq	4	3
Ivory Coast	5	1
Kenya	5	12
Kosovo	3	17
Lebanon	0	1
Liberia	2	2
Lithuania	1	2
Moldova	0	1
Nigeria	14	27
Pakistan	0	3
Poland	2	3
Romania	5	19
Russia	3	1
Rwanda	4	6
Senegal	0	1
Sierra Leone	16	3
Slovak Republic	0	2
Somalia	46	58
Sri Lanka	12	18
Sudan	1	2
Syria	0	1
Tanzania	6	26
Togo	1	1
Turkey	13	14
Turkish Rep of N Cyprus	1	0
Uganda	1	9
Ukraine	1	0
Zaire	13	15
Zambia	1	0
Total:	361	461

figures were recorded by the government for arrivals of un-accompanied children at ports of entry as well as in-country asylum applications: 192 in 1992; 274 in 1993; 404 in 1994; and 585 in 1995. These figures are all for children up to the age of 18 years. In 1996 there was a dramatic rise in the number of unaccompanied children seeking asylum in the UK, with figures doubling. This was mostly dur to young men fleeing human rights abuse in Kosovo.

It is also the case that identification of children as being unaccom-panied has very much improved since 1994. As a result of the Asylum and Immigration (Appeals) Act 1993, a duty was placed on the Secre-tary of State for the Home Office to establish a non-statutory Panel of Advisers for unaccompanied refugee children. This was subsequently set up at the Refugee Council. Immigration officers and staff at the Asylum Screening Unit at Lunar House, Croydon were instructed to refer any unaccompanied children to the Panel, and details of the Panel's services were widely distributed to other likely referral agencies, such as social services departments, refugee community organisations and legal representatives.

The Panel of Advisers started taking referrals in March 1994 and is now a key source of information regarding the age and gender (Table 4.1) as well as the country of origin of each child referred (Table 4.2). Numbers are affected by government policy. For example, when visa restrictions are imposed on nationals of certain countries, the number of asylum claims by unaccompanied children as well as by adults drop. Sierra Leone is a recent case in point.

It is clear from the Panel's work that the majority of unaccompanied refugee children referred are looked after by social services departments in London. Only a small number are referred from outside London (9% of the total to date), the majority of those being children who are detained in immigration detention facilities such as Campsfield (Oxfordshire) and HM Prisons Haslar (Hampshire) and Rochester (Kent).

'Unidentified' Children It is virtually certain that the total number, national and ethnic origin of unaccompanied refugee children in the United Kingdom is unknown. Some children travel with adults who appear to be their carers and they are thus not identified as being unaccompanied when they enter the country. They may or may not subsequently be identified as unaccompanied.

Local authority services for refugees generally, and unaccompanied children in particular, are seldom adequately publicised and are often more suitable to users from the host community. This has two consequences: first, refugees do not know what services are available and second, if they do, they may choose not to use them. Communities such as the Tamils often prefer to look after unaccompanied children in informal arrangements for this reason, as if the children were part of the family with whom they stay, and contact is not made with the relevant social services department.

Another reason for the non-identification of unaccompanied children is the uncertain immigration status of some refugee families with unrelated children living with them, whom they stated were their own children on arrival when making their asylum claim. They may not ask for assistance due to concern that the emergence of the truth will either jeopardise their own application for asylum or that of the unrelated children.

In communities such as the Somali community, clan and kinship ties and responsibilities are not light matters. Thus, many children unaccompanied by their usual carers – such as their parents – are looked after by 'aunts' and 'uncles' in the United Kingdom whom they have probably never met before coming here. Although the relationships are not those of 'aunt' and 'uncle' as narrowly defined in this country, they are nevertheless taken more seriously, and children will be brought up as part of the family.

An additional reason for incomplete statistics is that staff in social services departments which may be looking after unaccompanied children are not always well-informed about the asylum determination procedure. When the child is referred to them as being in need of accommodation because there is no-one with parental responsibility able to care for them in this country, they may not realise the child should make an asylum application. It is only when the child wishes to travel, start work or claim benefits that uncertain immigration status is identified. The Panel of Advisers has had several such referrals from social services departments, months or even years after the child has entered the country; how many other children are in the same position is not known for obvious reasons. It is also the case that many social services departments have not hitherto specified which children and young people they look after are unaccompanied refugees; in many cases where ethnic monitoring is carried out, it is not necessarily clear what a child's nationality is.

Schemes, convoys and adoption As mentioned above, some un-accompanied children arrive in the United Kingdom as a result of a 'pub-run', where concerned people plan rescue missions 'over a pint', and suddenly a local authority has a coach-load of asylum seekers – adults and children – on their hands with no provision made for them. There have been cases where children have been unaccompanied by any relative or familiar carer. There are similar schemes where groups of children are brought out of a war zone for 'a holiday' or for an extended 'study trip' while staying with host families. Social workers should consider the application of private fostering regulations in such situations for stays of over 28 days, and teachers should be aware of the many problems attendant on such schemes. 'Good practice' guidelines for such situations, include drawing attention to the need for proper documentation of children, prior formal granting of parental permission, arrangements for maintenance of contact, and so on. It should also be stressed that research on the subject points to the same conclusion: that because of the sense of security engendered by the presence of a trusted adult, children fare better with a familiar carer who is coping relatively well, even in dangerous circumstances, than if they are separated and 'taken to safety' on their own.

Social services departments need to be particularly vigilant when asked to consider the adoption of children from war zones or former war zones. As the 1994 UNHCR Guidelines on Refugee Children point out:

> Most unaccompanied minors are not orphans, and what they need is therefore reunification with their parents, not adoption. (United Nations High Commissioner for Refugees, 1994, p 130)

The recent case of Edita Keranovic, the Bosnian girl adopted by a British couple, whose adoption was set aside by a High Court judge illustrates this point all too well. Insufficient attempts were made to trace Edita's family, who were looking for her frantically. Although Edita is to remain in Britain, she is to retain her name and religion and must have contact with her grandfather at least four times a year (Daly, 1997).

The experiences of unaccompanied refugee children

Each child and young person will have their own story, and it is important not to make generalisations. However, children of particular nationalities are more likely to undergo a certain range of experiences, and it is important that adults working with them are familiar with these. To give just a few examples: children and young people from Eritrea and Ethiopia have generally experienced secure, intact family life before flight; those from Angola or Liberia often come from situations where family and community life has been disrupted for some time; many Somali refugees may well have spent considerable periods of time in large refugee camps, probably with no educational facilities.

Unaccompanied children are just as likely as other refugee children to have witnessed, or themselves experienced, destruction of homes and buildings as well as violence against individuals and communities. Or, like other refugee children, they may have been quite unaware of what was going on in their country until they had to leave. The difference, of course, is that from the beginning of, or during, their flight they are without familiar adults to protect, guide and interpret what is happening for them. They may also be in the unenviable position of having to fulfil those functions for younger siblings or family members entrusted to them.

The effect of being unaccompanied will, of course, vary according to the child's age and developmental maturity as well as to their pre-flight experiences, security and confidence. It should be recognised that the normal reactions of any child to being a refugee – survivor guilt, fear that it is 'all their fault', anger and anxiety that their parents could not protect them – are likely to be heightened for those children who, perhaps alone in their families, have arrived in a 'safe' country. A normal stage for any refugee to pass through is the transition from 'honeymoon period' to disappointment that the country of exile is not a problem-free safe haven. How much more complicated children who know that the whole family have made enormous sacrifices – both financial and of their safety – to enable them to come to 'a better life' in Britain if that better life turns out to be a misery? And what of the children who did not understand the dangers they faced because they had led a sheltered life, and who feel utterly rejected at being sent here because they do not understand the reason why? And how is it for those children whose parents could not bear to tell them the truth, and who pretended they would be travelling with them until the last moment? Or those whose parents genuinely believed they would be able to follow later, but cannot because of tighter visa controls?

The author is currently conducting research into policy-making and service provision for unaccompanied refugee children in four different London boroughs. Some 23 children and young people have been interviewed, as well as many of their carers and other professionals working with them. Although their nationalities and experiences before, during and after flight varied considerably, there was broad consensus among young people about their needs in this country. With a few variations, the majority agreed the following was necessary:

- caring, loving adults who will take time, in comfortable surroundings, to look underneath a coping exterior and help children understand why they are here

- adults who take the necessary details and keep them safe, so the young person does not have to repeat the story to different people

- having links with refugee community organisations to look for relatives and find ways of contacting home

- a good solicitor who gives them clear explanations of their legal situation

- having their own food and customs, or at least having adults around who are interested enough in their culture and history to find out about it

- teachers who are strict but fair, give extra help and expect young people to achieve what they are capable of – not necessarily what their peers are satisfied with achieving -because the teachers understand that failure is 'a disaster'

- careers advice that gives them a chance to think about all the options on offer, what they can realistically achieve and what will be of use back home;

- learning about British life, how to counter racism and different ways of solving conflict without the backing of their immediate family;

- plenty of activities to keep their minds off their problems and where they can mix with other young people, make friends and achieve something, for example through sport;

- sympathetic health workers who listen and explain carefully.

As well as unaccompanied refugee children not understanding the reasons for their flight to Britain, many may be quite unaware of the presence of other young people in the same situation as themselves or indeed, that it is nothing new for children to be sent to Britain – or away from Britain – to safety. Their sense of isolation is likely to be reduced if this can be explored by means of the normal curriculum, on an individual basis or better, in a group of similar young people.

Unaccompanied refugee children and the law

International law of particular importance to unaccompanied refugee children includes the 1951 UN Convention on the Status Relating to Refugees and the 1967 Protocol, the 1989 UN Convention on the Rights of the Child and law relating to adoption. While educationalists are not required to be experts in this field, it is nevertheless very helpful to have a working knowledge of relevant provisions. These are outlined in Chapter Two.

In Britain, it is important that those working with unaccompanied refugee children understand what their experience of claiming asylum involves, and particular measures which may affect them. More details of the asylum determination procedure and refusal and deportation are given in Chapter Two.

Once an asylum-seeking child has arrived at a British port of entry and has been given leave to enter the country by an Immigration Officer, they become subject to national laws. The most significant to unaccompanied children is the Children Act 1989 which provides the foundation for family and child care law in England and Wales.

The provisions of the Children Act are made within an overall framework of certain key concepts applicable to all children, but with considerable relevance to unaccompanied refugee children. For example, the 'paramount consideration' of the child's welfare [Section 1(1)] supports the view that refugee children should be treated as *children* with individual needs first and foremost, rather than being considered either as members of a homogeneous group or possibly as pawns in the wider world of politics. Any plans made should be shaped by the ascertainable wishes and feelings of the child [Section 1(3)]. In the case of unaccompanied refugee children, it must thus be ensured that the children really understand the nature of their rights and the choices open to them, and that their wishes and feelings are not only considered, but also understood, by adults. It is likely to be necessary to use skilled interpreters, familiar with the work of social services departments, who can explain to the child the role of the various authorities with whom they come into contact.

The Children Act further states – for the first time in child care or family law – that 'due consideration' must be given to a child's religious persuasion, racial origin and cultural and linguistic background in any plans made for that child [Section 74(6)]. This is obviously of enormous importance if refugee children who have already lost their closest family, friends, cultural milieu and homeland are not to suffer the further loss of their heritage and, indeed, their identity.

Another underlying principle is that of parental responsibility and that children are usually best cared for by their own families. The necessity is stressed for local authorities to work in partnership with parents and the child's wider family as well as with their community in Britain. In the case of unaccompanied refugee children, this should involve attempts to trace the children's parents or family members in this country or abroad to ascertain what their plans are, following advice as to whether this may jeopardise a family's safety. The Red Cross operates a Message and Tracing Service which can be helpful in this regard. Advocacy with the Home Office for family reunion in line with Article 10.1 of the UN Convention on the Rights of the Child may also be called for.

General provisions of the Children Act clearly include children who are unaccompanied refugees. Local authorities have a duty to provide accommodation for any child in their area who needs accommodation as a result of there being no-one who has parental responsibility for them, or who are lost and abandoned [Section 20(1)]. Any child thus 'accommodated' by a local authority, who has infrequent or no communication with someone who has parental responsibility for them, has the right to have an 'Independent Visitor' appointed to advise, befriend, and if necessary advocate for them (Schedule 2 #17). Local authorities have powers to provide accommodation for young people between the ages of 16 and 21 if they consider that to do so will safeguard and promote their welfare, and they have a duty to accommodate a child in their area who has reached the age of 16 and who is deemed to be 'in need' as defined by the Act [Section 20(3)]. There are also extended duties and powers in respect of after-care [Sections 20, 24 and 27; 61 and 64] which should ensure that a stronger safety net is in place for all those young people no longer looked after by local authorities, of whom refugee young people must surely be among the most vulnerable. Support, financial or in kind, can be provided under Section 11 to children 'in need'.

The Children Act 1989 unfortunately did not close the loophole in previous child care law concerning the question of who can have parental responsibility for unaccompanied refugee children whose parents it has not been possible to consult. This matter remains largely unresolved except in those cases where a local authority takes care proceedings and a Care Order is made in respect of an unaccompanied child. Teachers who have taken a particular interest in a child or young person who is unaccompanied have sometimes acted 'in loco parentis' (in place of a parent), for example, by signing consent forms for medical treatment. However, this is highly inappropriate because of legal difficulties should something go wrong; such matters should be referred to the social services department concerned.

Practice guidance for social workers In recognition of the lack of specialised knowledge about, and training for, working with refugees, particularly unaccompanied refugee children, draft practice guidelines were drawn up by the Department of Health to be published in 1991 in conjunction with the other volumes of guidance accompanying the Children Act. Regrettably there was a delay of several years, but the Training Pack and Practice Guide on Unaccompanied Asylum-seeking Children was finally published by the Social Services Inspectorate of the Department of Health in May 1995 (Department of Health, 1995a and 1995b). Although addressed specifically to social workers, the Practice Guide is important reading for others concerned with the welfare of unaccompanied children so that they are clear what is expected of social services departments. In addition, much information is provided which is useful for other professionals working with unaccompanied children on subjects such as working in partnership with refugee community organisations, confidentiality and working with interpreters and other key areas.

Different responses of social services departments

A local authority's responsibilities towards those children living in its area of jurisdiction are clearly outlined in the Children Act 1989. However, some local authority Social Service Departments have been reluctant to accept responsibility for unaccompanied refugee children referred to them for assistance, on the grounds that the children's needs should have been assessed and met by the authority either where the child first entered the country or somewhere else they have stayed recently. Prior to the Children Act 1989 coming into force, the Social Services Inspectorate of the Department of Health had already addressed this specific problem in a letter from Bill Utting, Chief Inspector, which was sent to all Directors of Social Services in the country on 23 January 1991. It was made clear:

> ...the local authority for the area in which an abandoned child...is physically present when his or her 'unaccompanied' situation comes to the attention of social services has a duty to receive the child into its care if this is necessary in the interests of the welfare of the child.

63

In other words, it is not just those local authorities where there are ports or airports who must shoulder the responsibility for unaccompanied refugee children. Indeed, if the children have lived in a certain community before the authority becomes aware that they are unaccompanied, they are certain to have made at least some links within that community and so it would be inappropriate to move them to the area where they first entered the country. Consequently, unaccompanied refugee children are to be found in every single local authority in London, although in varying numbers.

During the autumn of 1992, the author conducted a survey of service provision for unaccompanied refugee children in the 33 London boroughs, Essex and West Sussex. Of the 28 local authority social services departments who responded to the survey, several were looking after more than 10 unaccompanied refugee children, namely: Brent (11), Camden (42), Croydon (10), Ealing (15), Hackney (11), Hammersmith and Fulham (23), Haringey (38), Hillingdon (41), Hounslow (19), Kensington and Chelsea (50), Lambeth (47), Newham (13) and Westminster (14). West Sussex County Council, where Gatwick is situated, was looking after 11 children. Three years later, most authorities had experienced an increase in the number of unaccompanied children who were looked after, largely because relatively few at that point had been discharged from care. The most significant exception is Hillingdon in which Heathrow Airport is situated, where numbers looked after remain fairly constant, although the total number of individual children in a year is much higher. This is because the social services department has been successful in identifying relatives or friends of the children living elsewhere in London, of whom the children often have no prior knowledge, but with whom they are able to live after investigations are made.

Some authorities have been more willing to accept their responsibilities to unaccompanied refugee children under the Children Act than others. One difficulty has undoubtedly been the cost of looking after these children. Providing residential accommodation or foster care is always very expensive and unaccompanied refugee children often have particular needs which lead to additional costs – for example, needs which can best be met by the recruitment of staff and carers who speak their language.

One clear case is Hillingdon; many unaccompanied refugee children arrive at Heathrow and are identified there as being in need of assistance. In 1991, Hillingdon Social Services Department spent £967,000 on accommodating such children – no small sum to find in addition to that for planned expenditure – and the costs were met from the authority's reserves. In 1992, the community charge was increased to meet the expenditure, and Hillingdon was charge-capped. The Borough appealed, on the grounds that the expenditure relating to unaccompanied refugee children is not covered by the criteria on which Standard Spending Assessments are calculated, i.e. the number of children in need already living in a local authority. The appeal was lost, although a one-off payment was subsequently made to the London boroughs of Hillingdon and Kensington and Chelsea following strenuous representations. The issue has remained unresolved until a central government announcement early this year was made to the effect that £3 million would be made available through the Department of Health for the reimbursement of costs in relation to expenditure on unaccompanied refugee children.

The experience of Refugee Council members of the Panel of Advisers for Refugee Children is still that some social services departments are reluctant to take responsibility for unaccompanied refugee children – especially 16 and 17 year olds affected by the Social Security Regulations, changes incorporated within the Asylum and Immigration Act 1996, in spite of both the incontestable nature of the children's vulnerability and the clear directive issued by the Social Services Inspectorate. They try to argue that the children are the responsibility of some other authority where the children may have already stayed; while they are arguing, the children are left in limbo. Even where authorities do accept responsibility, provision varies greatly.

The Refugee Council has become concerned that bed and breakfast hotels are being increasingly used by social services departments to house 16 and 17 year old asylum-seekers – placements which are quite inappropriate. On the whole, unaccompanied refugee children and young people probably experience no better and no worse provision than the majority of other children and young people looked after by local authorities. Like them, they are on the receiving end of the change in policy towards family placement or fostering and away from long-term residential care – unless specialist provision is indicated – and within fostering, of the push for 'same race' placements – for example, Black children with Black foster carers. Far less attention has generally been given to children's actual nationality, culture, language and religion.

It is very unusual for a child under ten years of age to be accommodated in a children's home, unless they are with older siblings; the majority will be immediately placed with foster carers. Children between ten and 16 years when first accommodated by a social services department, will either be placed directly with foster carers, or more usually, in a children's home whose purpose is assessment. Depending on the outcome of the assessment, they are likely to be moved to a foster family or other residential establishment. However, if the plan is for them to have training for independent living fairly soon, they may continue to live in the children's home until a suitable place in a semi-independent unit becomes available.

The geographical location and type of foster care varies enormously. Some local authorities will be able to place children with local foster carers locally. Others may have been unable to recruit the type of foster carers they need within their own area and have looked further afield. In this way, a child who attends a particular school and lives with a local foster carer may have been placed there by a social services department some distance away. However, it is the placing authority's ongoing responsibility to monitor the placement, not the authority in which the placement is situated. As regards type of carer, while it is best practice to match a child to a family placement as close as possible in nationality, culture, religion, language and political affiliation as well as similarity to the structure of the child's birth family, this is not always possible – at least initially.

Some social services departments have invested considerable resources in recruiting foster carers from refugee communities, and are able to make quite good matches even for emergency placements. Some take considerable care in recruiting carers for specific children, once it has been agreed that their needs will best be met within a family setting. In some instances, social workers have been able to match children and families down to their clan and village of origin, as well as to the type of family, for example, headed by a woman or a man.

Other social services departments may be able to match placements according to region, for example, a Somali child with an Eritrean carer. Still others may be able to make matches only according to ethnicity or religion, for example an Angolan child with a Nigerian or Jamaican family, an Afghan child with a Pakistani family. In other cases, there may appear to have been very little consideration given to matching at all.

Sometimes such cross-cultural placements work well and the children concerned settle happily, but even the best-matched placements are likely to experience difficulties. It is not an easy job to bring up children who have had very difficult experiences and who are suffering enormous loss, nor is it easy for a child to accept the discipline, care and routine of a strange family when they want to be with their own family and perhaps do not understand why they have to be in Britain to start with.

The type of children's homes also varies. Most local authorities have reduced the number of children's homes which they operate them-selves, and for some children they use placements in children's homes run by the private and voluntary sector. As with foster placements, these homes may or may not be situated within a placing authority's boundaries but the placing authority continues to have responsibility for the children placed out of borough.

Where close matching of family placements is not possible, or where children are living in residential care without adults from their own community around them, the importance of maintaining culture, language and religious practice is vital. Attendance at supplementary schools, cultural and religious events is clearly even more important than for refugee children living with their families.

Where changes in placement are planned, including those planned from day one as in the case of children placed inappropriately in residential care because of a lack of emergency foster placements, the vast majority of unaccompanied refugee children are extremely reluctant to move. Even where their placement is patently unsuitable, for example, with no adult speaking their language, they will often resist leaving especially if this also means a change in school. This reluctance is common among many looked-after children but is heightened in the case of unaccompanied children who wish to cling onto the very first experience of some security following their flight. They need considerable support to make the transition, and a longer 'introduction period' to the new carer is often helpful.

16-17 year olds In the case of young people over the age of 16 years referred to social services departments, policies vary considerably among local authorities. In some cases, their vulnerability is fully appreciated by social services departments and they may be accommodated in foster or residential care, or in some form of supported living. In the majority of others, they are expected to manage with little help, and may be placed immediately in a hostel or bed and breakfast accommodation. While a minority of social services departments have proved reluctant to take any financial responsibility for 16 and 17 year olds since the Social Security Regulation changes it is nevertheless possible to argue that they have a duty to assess the young person's situation, and that in accordance with Section 20 of the Children Act, they have a duty to provide accommodation if the young person is in need and if their welfare is likely to be seriously prejudiced without the provision of services. However, in most cases, these young people are only given financial support under Section 17 to live independently, with no ongoing social work assistance.

Where young people have been accommodated before they are 16, they usually continue being accommodated until they are 17 or 18 years. They will then be assisted to find independent accommodation or may be referred to semi-independent provision. As care leavers, they will benefit from their social services department's arrangements for after care, and if they are intending to pursue full-time education, social services has an obligation to support them until their studies are completed.

Young carers Sometimes groups of siblings live together, with a 19 or 20 year old looking after several younger children and having to cope single-handed with a completely strange system as well as their own and their siblings' losses and needs. These young families often do not come to the attention of social services until the eldest carer reaches breaking point, at which juncture the young siblings may need to be accommodated.

Informal carers and social services departments A similar situation can occur with families who are caring for children unrelated to them, but with friendship or clan ties. Sometimes an unaccompanied child can simply have travelled with that family en route to Britain, and remains in their care after arrival. Strictly speaking, such caring relationships should be regarded as private fostering arrangements, and thus subject to monitoring by social services departments, but in practice this is rare. Because of the stresses and strains many asylum-seeking families are under with housing, health and other problems it can be the unaccompanied child who is rejected when the going gets too tough, or indeed, the child or young person may simply not accept the authority of an adult who is not closely related to him or her. Very often these families do not know about services which could lessen the stress they are under, such as day care or play facilities for younger children in the family or the advice and support available from social workers. Social services departments are seeing more such cases where removal from the family is the only option.

A matter of concern which has come to the attention of some refugee community organisations is that of unaccompanied refugee children being cared for in informal arrangements, who are moved from family to family. Their schooling is often interrupted as a result and they may not necessarily be treated well.

Placement with relatives After arriving in Britain some unaccompanied refugee children are linked up with relatives already settled here, whom they may or may not have known back home, often with the help of refugee community organisations. Where the arrangement is assessed to be satisfactory, an unaccompanied child is likely to go to live with them. There is no statutory requirement for ongoing monitoring of situations where close family ties are concerned, and after the child is settled and immediate practical matters are sorted out, a social services department will probably not have further involvement.

Inter-agency co-operation and planning

The Children Act 1989 laid two new duties on local authorities regarding planning. The powers and duties required of local authorities under the Children Act are assigned to Social Services Committees (Local Authority Social Services Act 1970), but under Section 27, other local authority departments and health authorities are required to co-operate in providing services if the request to do so is not incompatible with the discharge of their other functions. Local education authorities and social services departments are also specifically required jointly to carry out reviews of all day care services for children under eight in their area at least once every three years (Section 19).

Following publication of the inquiry report by Staffordshire County Council on the 'Pindown' regime in children's residential care, the government commissioned a national review of residential care for children, the conclusions of which were published in the Utting Report (1991). One of the recommendations was that social services departments should draw up a Children's Services Plan. The Department of Health subsequently issued Circular LAC(92)18 which outlined its expectations of such plans, making clear that they should be the product of collaboration between local authorities (including local education authorities), health authorities, voluntary organisations, the private sector and other appropriate interests.

Local authorities carry out this planning in different ways. Many have chosen to form multi-disciplinary task groups focusing on different age groups of children and/or children with particular needs, for example, children with disabilities or children who are looked after by the local authority. In only a few instances have refugee children been the subject of such a focus.

A multi-disciplinary focus on 'looked after' children and young people generally is certainly overdue. The Department of Health and OFSTED have published a joint report on just this subject containing much sensible advice (Department of Health/OFSTED, 1995). There is considerable evidence that these young people's educational needs have all too often been overlooked. Sonia Jackson (Jackson, 1988) has clearly identified how children in care underperform educationally. Factors leading to poor attainment include the prioritisation of welfare above educational concerns, especially when placement moves are being organised and disruption in education is caused by placement moves (cf. also Biehal et al, 1992).

Planning for refugee children and young people

Since the Social Services Inspectorate (London Region) of the Department of Health began convening the 'Network on Children and Families from Abroad' in 1995, all social services departments in London have designated a lead officer so some improvement can be expected. However, not all social services departments are clear how many children and young people looked after are refugees, whether unaccompanied or otherwise. The Network has recently drawn up an agreed format for monitoring unaccompanied refugee children and the services provided them, and it is to be hoped that this will lead to a clearer picture of the population and distribution of refugee children throughout London.

Any local authority Children's Services Plan should consider the needs of refugee young people as part of their strategy for looked after young people. The planning process outlined above should cover the provision of appropriate systems and resources for the careful assessment of unaccompanied refugee children, including assessment of their educational needs. As the parents cannot be consulted about a child's educational history and achievements, more weight will have to be given to the input of the child, as well as that of older siblings or members of the child's community who may be familiar with the particular schools they attended.

In addition, there should be careful planning when care packages which include an educational input are devised and reviewed. Schools and educational psychologists will have an important role to play here, as will refugee community organisations. All concerned should be familiar with the statutory requirements for reviews outlined in the Review of Children's Cases Regulations 1991, particularly with regard to timing (within four weeks of first being looked after, then after three months and subsequently at intervals of no more than six months).

The experience of many working with refugee children, whether accompanied or not, has been that underachievement is a significant contributor to stress and psychological ill-health, particularly for those who arrive in Britain at an age where they cannot possibly catch up with their British counterparts. It is likely to be even more significant for unaccompanied children, for whom education has become the be-all of their existence and may be their only compensation for the unhappiness they experience in being separated from their families. Utting has pointed out of children looked after: 'Educational attainment is one means by which children will be strengthened to cope with independence' (Utting, 1991). As has already been indicated in earlier chapters, education and educational attainment are important contributory factors assisting the reintegration of identity in exile and the successful creation of a new life in Britain (cf. for example, Rutter, 1985). Education authorities need to provide clear guidance for foster carers and residential staff working with refugee children as to how they can support children's educational aspirations and career plans.

Recommendations for good practice in education
Local authorities should commit themselves to upholding and implementing the principles and standards of the UN Convention on the Rights of the Child.

Identifying unaccompanied refugee children in schools
- When admitting new pupils, ensure staff are aware of the wide range of caring arrangements for refugee children which include living in a children's home, with foster carers, older siblings or members of the community. This information should be noted carefully, and brought to the attention of the class teacher and other relevant adults

- Where children are living with adults unrelated to them, ensure the social services department is informed – with the knowledge of the family – so they can assess whether private fostering regulations apply

- Ensure sibling or relative carers are aware of support available from the social services department

- Be sensitive to the exclusive language and thinking sometimes used in schools, such as letters to 'parents/guardians', 'parents' evenings' as well as to the timing of school events for those with caring responsibilities.

Support in the asylum determination procedure

- Be aware an unaccompanied refugee child may not have had appropriate legal advice about making an asylum claim, even if looked after by a social services department

- Never contact the Home Office directly on behalf of a child or help them make their asylum claim – contact a legal adviser

- Ensure a child knows about the Refugee Council's Panel of Advisers, and help them make contact if they wish

- Ensure staff understand about the process of making an asylum claim, so they can support the child at particularly difficult times, for example following a refusal or through the appeals process

- Consider making a report to support the child's claim, and ensure the legal representative knows the school will do this.

School curriculum and pastoral role

- Be sensitive in particular subjects to the fact that not all pupils live with their parents

- Ensure that the phenomena of evacuees and unaccompanied refugee children are included in any treatment of refugee issues or certain periods of history, such as the Spanish Civil War, Second World War, including autobiographical accounts (e.g. Gershon, 1989; Statler, 1990 and Wicks, 1989)

- Find out about the likely reasons why there are unaccompanied refugee children from particular countries in the school

- Recognise the added importance of teachers/headteachers playing a parental role, both in terms of advice and authority, in such areas as praise for achievement, understanding their experience before and after flight, help in conflict resolution, further education and careers advice and so on

- As with any other child, teachers need to be aware that an un-accompanied refugee child might be abused and may need protection.

- Ensure unaccompanied refugee children know about the Red Cross Tracing and Message Services

- Be alert to the existence of 'holiday schemes' or 'respite care' for children from war zones, and ensure that the local social services department is aware of them.

'Looked after' children

- Have access to Department of Health Social Services Inspectorate practice guidance on unaccompanied asylum-seeking children (Department of Health, 1995a)

- Ensure staff are clear about the local authority's policy for looked-after children in general and refugee children in particular

- Enable staff to participate in care planning and statutory reviews

- Be prepared to challenge poor practice and to complain on behalf of a child who is not getting a good service or not being listened to by social services.

Concluding comments on links between education and social services

There should already be a named person at senior management level in every local education authority who has overall responsibility for looked-after children, including the following responsibilities:

- close liaison with a named person at senior management level in the social services department concerning 'looked-after' children and young people

- the consideration of any policy or practice issues arising from this;

- ensuring that care and attention is given to the education, career development and working life of children 'looked after' by any social services department, but who are being educated locally.

* Hansard, House of Commons, Vol 216, no 96, cols 103-4, Written Answers 15 December 1992. Statistics were initially for children under 16 years and only those identified at port of entry, subsequently years' figures being for children up to the age of 18 years and both port and in-country cases.

CHAPTER FIVE

The Psychological Adaptation of Refugee Children

William Yule

Introduction

With the ending of the 'Cold War' between the superpowers, the world is now realising that there are many local wars that give rise to real misery. The rise in nationalism and the civil wars associated with ethnic conflict throughout the world are characterised by vicious targeting of the civilian population. UNICEF recently estimated that over 80 per cent of the victims of today's warfare are women and children. Civilian populations are deliberately targeted; 'ethnic cleansing' and massacres are almost commonplace; populations are held hostage and under siege; even international economic sanctions are used as weapons in the struggles.

Against this background, it is clear that many children suffer. Studies supported by UNICEF in the former Yugoslavia found that in towns and cities such as Sarajevo, Mostar, Tuzla and Zenica in Bosnia, almost all the children reported that they had experienced shells and grenades exploding near them. Most children believed they had been the targets of sniper fire. Half the children said that they had seen the bodies of people killed in the fighting, and, indeed, half of those had actually witnessed the killing. In the bitter winter of 1994, children in Sarajevo worried about dying of cold and hunger. The greater the number of adverse, war-related events the children reported, the more likely they were to report distressing symptoms of stress.

Whether it be in Vietnam, Cambodia, Rwanda or Bosnia, these modern wars result in many families with young children fleeing to safety. 'Ethnic cleansing' in Yugoslavia deliberately caused hundreds of thousands of people to leave the places they grew up in to try to find safety elsewhere. Simply to escape the fighting and risk of reprisal, people uproot themselves and seek refuge in other countries. The result is that it has been estimated that there are over 19 million people who are refugees (within the formal meaning of the term as defined by the 1951 UN Convention Relating to the Status of Refugees) with a further 27 million people living in refugee-like situations of internal displacement but not having crossed any international border (Rutter, 1994). It does not take much imagination to think of the experiences children may have had in fleeing from their homes under threat, witnessing fighting and destruction, seeing violent acts directed at their loved ones, leaving their friends and possessions behind, marching or being transported in crowded vehicles, spending months in transit camps and eventually finding temporary respite in a country at peace while the authorities decide whether the family can be granted permission to remain legally and indefinitely.

Put this way, it can be seen that the experiences that many refugee children have faced are contrary to what most people consider to be the basic needs of every child: the need for continuity of care by a loved one; the need for shelter and food; the need for safety and security; the need for good schooling. All these are compromised. One has only to read the Declaration of Amsterdam – *The Declaration and Recommendations on the Rights of Children in Armed Conflict* adopted by consensus at a meeting in Amsterdam on 21 June 1994 (Aldrich and van Baarda, 1994) to appreciate how difficult it becomes to meet the needs of children displaced in such dreadful circumstances.

At present, there seems to be no end to the number of bitter local wars that result in children being displaced from their homes, with or without their families. It means that most Western European countries have a sizeable number of refugee children living within them, and the UK is no exception. Most large cities have known refugee communities within them, and in London, there can scarcely be a school that does not have some refugee children on roll. The educational needs of these children have been recognised for a long time (Rutter, 1994), even if they are not always adequately met. Meeting the child's educational needs and providing a semblance of stability in part of their daily life is an important aspect of meeting their overall mental health needs. Thus, this chapter will examine some of the responses of refugee children to their losses and the traumatic events that have befallen them, and examines some of the ways that education, health and social services can work with other community based agencies to provide emotional support to refugee children.

Stress reactions in children

Research carried out in the last ten years has shown that children react to life threatening stressors in various ways (Yule, 1991, 1994). Depression, anxiety, fears and bereavement reactions, as well as Post Traumatic Stress Disorders (PTSD) can occur. The form of PTSD varies according to the age of the child and, sadly, the internal distress often goes unrecognised for long periods by parents and teachers. Indeed, one of the reasons that there was doubt until recently as to whether PTSD occurred in children was that few investigators had asked the children themselves how they were affected.

For centuries major stress reactions have been known to occur and it is ironic that it has been in the aftermath of major wars that our understanding of people's reactions to life-threatening experiences has been advanced. It was not until the persisting problems of Vietnam veterans were better documented that it was realised that three major groups of symptoms – distressing recurring recollections of the traumatic event; avoidance of stimuli associated with the trauma; and a range of signs of increased physiological arousal – formed a coherent syndrome that came to be labelled Post Traumatic Stress Disorder (PTSD) (Horowitz, 1976; APA, 1980).

PTSD is classified in formal psychiatric diagnostic schemes as an anxiety disorder. It was increasingly described as 'a normal reaction to an abnormal situation', and so, logically, it was queried whether it should be regarded as a psychiatric disorder at all (O'Donohue and Eliot, 1992). Indeed, debate still rages as to whether such a 'disorder' can legitimately be diagnosed in people from different cultures.

However, for present purposes, it provides a useful framework within which to examine children's reactions to major stressors.

It is, of course, not only the 'objective' nature of the stressful experience that matters, but how the child subjectively interprets that experience. There can be wide individual differences in reactions to what, to the outsider, may appear to be very similar experiences. There have been relatively few studies of the effects of major trauma on children so that the full range of post traumatic symptoms and their prevalence at different ages are not clearly established. The psychiatric classificatory systems of the American Psychiatric Association (The Diagnostic and Statistical Manual or DSM, APA, 1994) and the World Health Organisation's International Classification of Diseases (ICD, WHO, 1994) both provide diagnostic criteria that have been valuable in focusing the attention of researchers and clinicians on the disorder but there is still a need for careful descriptive studies of representative groups of traumatised children to establish the natural history of the disorder in children.

Following my experience of assessing and working with child and adolescent survivors of the capsize of the *Herald of Free Enterprise* car ferry (Yule and Williams, 1990) and those from the sinking of the cruise ship, *Jupiter*, (Yule, Udwin and Murdoch, 1990; Yule, 1992a), I noted the following common reactions:

Most children are troubled by *repetitive, intrusive thoughts* about the accident. Such thoughts can occur at any time, but particularly when the children are otherwise quiet, as when they are trying to drop off to sleep. At other times, the thoughts and vivid recollections are triggered off by reminders in their environment. Vivid *flashbacks* are not uncommon. *Sleep disturbances* are very common, particularly in the first few weeks. *Fears* of the dark and bad dreams, *nightmares*, and waking through the night are widespread.

Separation difficulties are frequent, even among teenagers. For the first few days, children may not want to let their parents out of their sight, even reverting to sleeping in the parental bed. Many children become much more *irritable and angry* than previously, both with parents and peers.

Although child survivors experience a *pressure to talk* about their experiences, paradoxically they also find it very *difficult to talk with their parents and peers*. Often they do not want to upset the adults and so parents may not be aware of the full extent of their children's suffering. Peers may hold back from asking what happened in case they upset the child further; the survivor often feels this as a rejection.

Children report a number of *cognitive changes*. Many experience *difficulties in concentration*, especially in school work. Others report *memory problems*, both in grasping new material and in remembering old skills such as reading music. They become very *alert to danger* in their environment, being adversely affected by reports of other disasters.

Survivors have learned that life is very fragile. This can lead to a loss of faith in the future or a *sense of foreshortened future*. Their priorities change. Some feel they should live each day to the full and not plan far ahead. Others realise they have been over-concerned with materialistic or petty matters and resolve to rethink their values. Their 'assumptive world' has been challenged (Janoff-Bulman, 1985).

Not surprisingly, many develop *fears* associated with specific aspects of their experiences. They avoid situations they associate with the disaster. Many experience *'survivor guilt'* – about surviving when others died; about thinking they should have done more to help others; about what they themselves did to survive.

Adolescent survivors report significantly high rates of depression, some becoming clinically depressed, having suicidal thoughts and taking overdoses in the year after a disaster. A significant number become very anxious after accidents, although the appearance of *panic attacks* is sometimes considerably delayed. When children have been bereaved, they may need bereavement counselling.

In summary, children and adolescents surviving a life-threatening disaster show a wide range of symptoms which tend to cluster around signs of re-experiencing the traumatic event, trying to avoid dealing with the emotions that this gives rise to, and a range of signs of increased physiological arousal. There may be considerable co-morbidity with depression, generalised anxiety or pathological grief reactions.

In younger children, parents and teachers initially report that they do not easily talk about the trauma. Recent experience has been that many young children easily give graphic accounts of their experiences and were also able to report how distressing the re-experiencing in thoughts and images was (Sullivan, Saylor and Foster, 1991; Misch, Phillips, Evans and Berelowitz, 1993). Pre-school children show much more regressive behaviour as well as more anti-social, aggressive and destructive behaviour. There are many anecdotal accounts of pre-school children showing repetitive drawing and play involving themes about the trauma they experienced. Many writers agree that it is very difficult to elicit evidence of emotional numbing in children (Frederick, 1985). Many do show loss of interest in activities and hobbies that previously gave them pleasure.

All clinicians and researchers need to have a good understanding of children's development to be able to assist them express their inner distress.

The nature of the traumatic event

It is clear that not everyone responds to the same trauma with identical symptoms. In part, these responses may be constitutionally determined; in part, they may be determined by the different ways people interpret the threats to themselves. Thus, as Rachman (1980) argued, one has to take into account both the objective and the subjective factors when trying to understand why any particular individual has such difficulties processing emotional reactions. The result may be PTSD.

There are four sets of studies of children's reactions to threat and disaster that show strong exposure-effect relationships. In the first, following the California school sniper attack, Pynoos and his colleagues (Pynoos and Eth, 1986; Pynoos, Frederick, Nader, Arroyo, Steinberg, Eth, Nunez and Fairbanks, 1987; Pynoos and Nader, 1988) investigated 159 children whose average age was 9.2 years (14.5 per cent of those attending the school) and who were exposed to a sniper attack on the school in which one child and a passer-by were killed and thirteen other children were injured. Nearly 40 per cent of the children were found to have moderate to severe PTSD. There was a very strong relationship between exposure and later effects in that those children who were trapped in the playground scored much higher than those who had left the vicinity of the school before the attack or were not in school that day.

In a fourteen month follow-up study, Nader, Pynoos, Fairbanks and Frederick (1991) reported that 74 per cent of the most severely exposed children in the playground still reported moderate to severe levels of PTSD, contrasting with 81 per cent of the unexposed children reporting no PTSD. Earlier Post Traumatic Stress Reaction Index scores were strongly related to those obtained at follow-up. In this study, the moderating effects of families' reactions was not reported but the strength of the relationships noted challenges McFarlane's (1987) claim that most effects are mediated by parental reaction.

In the second study, following the 1988 Armenian earthquake, Pynoos, Goenjian *et al* (1993) used the Post Traumatic Stress Reaction Index in translation with three groups of children – one from a town at the epicentre where buildings were totally demolished, one from a town at the periphery of the devastation, and one control group from outside the affected area. There was a clear exposure-effect relationship, with the most exposed children reporting highest scores.

The third study was of a British disaster. Five months after the sinking of the cruise ship, Jupiter, with over 400 British school children on board, Yule, Udwin and Murdoch (1990) studied self reported fears, anxiety and depression in a party of 24 adolescent girls from one school. Compared to girls who had wanted to go on the cruise (but did not get a place), other girls in the same school who expressed no interest in the cruise (but may have been upset by subsequent events) and controls from a similar school elsewhere, a 'subjective exposure'/ response effect was found for depression and anxiety but not for reported fears.

The final study again comes from the USA. Hurricane Hugo hit the eastern seaboard of the USA just north of Charleston, South Carolina on 21 September 1989. Lonigan et al (1991) received self-report data from 5,687 children and adolescents aged nine to 19 years. Degree of exposure was significantly associated with increased scores on both anxiety and stress reaction. Girls scored significantly higher than boys on both scales. The percentage showing mild, moderate or severe PTSD, as categorised on their total Stress Reaction Index Scores, was also highly related to the degree of exposure, being 5.06 per cent in the no exposure group, 10.35 per cent in the mild, 15.54 per cent in the moderate and 28.95 per cent in the high exposure group. The average anxiety scores for the hurricane survivors were much lower than those obtained from the 334 survivors of the Jupiter sinking (Yule 1992a) suggesting that the hurricane was less of a direct threat to the children.

Thus, within a single disaster, there is a strong relationship between degree of exposure to the stressor and subsequent adjustment. However, subjective factors also play a role. Studies of adult survivors find that high levels of pathology are related to the belief that the survivors were going to die during the incident, as well as to the experience of seeing dead and mutilated bodies (Williams, Joseph and Yule, 1992). Similar findings are emerging from the study of the most severely affected children assessed individually after the sinking of the Jupiter (Yule, Bolton and Udwin, 1992).

It should also be noted that where investigators use the same measures of post traumatic distress, this permits direct comparison between the studies. In turn, one can then see that disasters that differ in terms of severity or type may produce differing degrees of morbidity, which is in accordance with the model put forward by Rachman (1980). Thus, the scores on the Impact of Events Scale among survivors of the *Herald of Free Enterprise* capsize are higher than those of survivors of the *Jupiter* sinking. The former disaster was much more sudden and involved greater loss of life than the latter, suddenness and degree of life threat being two of Rachman's (1980) predictors of difficulties in emotional processing. In turn, both of these disasters gave rise to greater distress than did Hurricane Hugo (Lonigan et al, 1991), where loss of life was fortunately low, or the explosion at Lockerbie following the terrorist bombing of the Pan Am flight (Parry Jones et al, 1992).

In data emerging from UNICEF supported studies in Bosnia and Rwanda, again there is a clear relationship between the levels of stressful experiences reported by the children and the levels of subjective distress they also report. As noted earlier, parents and teachers do not always pick up the children's distress. This may be because of a number of complicated factors. Undoubtedly, adults often do not want to imagine what horrors children have experienced and so prefer not to ask about them. Children can be very sensitive to adults' reactions and if they sense that adults are upset by what they are telling them, they stop talking about it. Following the Australian bush fires, many teachers refused to complete behaviour rating scales on the children two years later in case that upset the children (McFarlane, Policansky and Irwin, 1987). While this illustrates a major dilemma faced by everyone working with traumatised children – when to talk about the traumatic event and when to avoid it – a moment's thought reveals that a teacher completing a questionnaire about a child need never reveal to the child that the event is being reconsidered. The refusal tells us more about the teachers' reactions than those of the children!

Among the implications of these findings for teachers working with refugee children is that they should find out as much as possible about the experiences the children had when leaving their country of origin. The more traumatic events they may have witnessed, the more likely it is that children will have difficulties settling in a new environment. Apart from the culture shock of arriving in a new society or even the obvious difficulties in mastering a new language, children may reveal their inner distress through such behaviours as poor concentration, difficulties in remembering things and a preoccupation with their own thoughts. At times, they may be very jumpy or irritable, even to the point of being aggressive. By understanding the level of traumatic experiences, such behaviours can be better understood in context.

Risk and protective factors
From all these studies, the following risk and protective factors (more fully discussed in Yule, 1992b) can be identified:

Age There are too few studies to examine whether children of different ages are at different risk of developing PTSD. The form of the disorder may vary with age, with children under six being more likely than older children to show repetitive play and drawing of the trauma (Terr, 1988; Yule, 1991). Age was not found to correlate with Stress Reaction Index scores in the Armenian earthquake (Pynoos et al, 1993). However,

Keppel-Benson and Ollendick (1993) note that young children's cognitive development will influence their interpretation of traumatic events as well as their ability to report symptoms. Thus, very young children may not be fully aware of the realistic threat of harm to themselves and so may be protected from strong emotional reactions. However, this should not be assumed as children vary markedly in their understanding of danger and death.

Sex Gibbs (1989) concludes that females are more vulnerable to the effects of disasters than males. This was confirmed in studies of the *Jupiter* sinking (Yule, 1992a), where girls scored higher than boys on anxiety, depression and fears as well as on the Horowitz et al (1979) Impact of Events Scale; in Hurricane Hugo (Lonigan et al, 1991); and in the Armenian earthquake (Pynoos et al, 1993). Contradictory findings are reported by Burke et al (1986) and (1982). In their earlier study they reported that six year old boys were more affected by floods and blizzards than girls but that in the fifth grade (age 10), girls were more affected than boys. Following the 1973 Yom Kippur war, Milgram and Milgram (1976) reported increased anxiety in Israeli boys but not in girls.

Ability Given that poor concentration and difficulties with new learning are said to be characteristic of PTSD, one might expect that children's school work would suffer after a disaster. Martin and Little (1986) investigated this following a tornado in Wichita Falls in April 1979 and failed to show any meaningful differences across the groups. Girls who survived the sinking of the Jupiter were above average in attainment during the three years prior to the cruise but their attainment plummeted significantly to merely average levels one year after the accident. Two years after the accident, in their GCSE results, the survivors still performed less well than expected, although the difference was no longer as marked (Tsui, Dagwell and Yule, forthcoming). Two other factors need to be emphasised. In the same group of adolescent girls studied by Tsui et al (Ibid.), Yule and Udwin (1991) had identified ten girls as being at higher risk than others solely on the basis of self-completed screening questionnaires. It was found that these high risk girls had significantly *lower* pre-accident attainment. Thus, lower attainment can be seen as a high risk factor, and higher attainment, and by implication higher ability, can be seen as a protective factor in this group. Thus, the experience of a major disaster can have an adverse effect on scholastic attainment. If this occurs at a crucial examination time, there may well be long term consequences. Schools must plan ahead with mental health and social services to ensure that any effects of a major crises are minimised (Yule and Gold, 1993).

School factors Many schools were affected by the *Jupiter* sinking and 334 pupils were screened on the same battery (Yule, 1992a). It was therefore possible to compare one school that accepted the offer of outside help with one that chose to cope on its own internal resources. Pupils in the school that accepted help showed slightly lower scores on anxiety and depression five months after the accident, and significantly lower scores on a fear survey schedule and the Impact of Events Scale. This provides some suggestive evidence for the value of early intervention as well as suggesting that how schools react to disasters is important in managing distress.

Family factors Following the Australian bush fires, it was found that families were affected, particularly in respect of increased levels of conflict and increased levels of maternal overprotection (McFarlane, 1987). Where parents had difficulties processing their own emotional reactions, they were less successful in helping their children. Those families who found it difficult to share their immediate reactions had more difficulties coming to terms with the disaster. Child and adolescent survivors of the *Herald of Free Enterprise* and *Jupiter* sinkings found it difficult to confide their inner feelings to their parents, in part to protect the parents from getting upset (Yule and Williams, 1990; Yule, 1991).

The Treatment of Stress Reactions
Crisis intervention: critical incident stress debriefing Debriefing was originally developed to assist emergency personnel adjust to their emotional reactions to events encountered in the course of their rescue work. It makes use of group support techniques within a predominantly male, macho culture where expressing and sharing feelings is not the norm. The technique has now been adapted for use with children

following a wide variety of traumas (Dyregrov, 1991). However, the very nature of refugee children's experiences in flight and exile means that it is unlikely that classical debriefing techniques will be used in the place of sanctuary. Even so, the technique is nowadays so widely discussed following a major incident that for the sake of completeness it is described here.

Within a few days of an incident, the survivors are brought together in a group with an outside leader. During the introductory phase, the leader sets the rules for the meeting emphasising that they are there to share feelings and help each other, and that what goes on in the meeting is private. The information should not be used to tease other children. No one has to talk, although all are encouraged to do so. They then go on to clarify the facts of what actually happened in the incident. This permits the nailing of any rumours. They are asked about what they thought when they realised something was wrong and this leads naturally into discussions of how they felt and of their current emotional reactions. In this way, children share the various reactions they have experienced and usually learn that others feel similarly. The leader labels their responses as normal (understandable) reactions to an abnormal situation. Many children are relieved to learn they are not the only ones experiencing strange feelings and so are relieved that there is an explanation and that they are not going mad. The leader summarises the information arising in the group, and educates the children into what simple steps they can take to control some of their reactions. They are also told of other help available should their distress persist.

There is evidence that this structured crisis intervention is helpful in preventing later distress in adults (Dyregrov, 1988; Duckworth, 1986; Robinson and Mitchell, 1993). Yule and Udwin (1991) describe their use of such debriefing with girls who survived the sinking of the Jupiter. Self-report data five months after the incident suggest that this reduced levels of stress, particularly those manifested in intrusive thoughts (Yule, 1992a). Stallard and Law (1993) show more convincing evidence that debriefing greatly reduced the distress of girls who survived a school bus crash. However, we still do not know when best to offer debriefing to survivors of a disaster, nor indeed whether all survivors benefit.

Group treatment Where natural groupings exist in communities and schools, it makes sense to direct some therapeutic support through such groups. (Galante and Foa, 1986; Farberow and Gordon, 1981; Ayalon, 1988; Yule and Williams, 1990; Yule and Udwin, 1991). The aims of such therapeutic groups should include the sharing of feelings, boosting children's sense of coping and mastery, sharing ways of solving common problems. Although no examples have been published to date, it would seem appropriate to offer group treatment to refugees who have experienced broadly similar events.

Gillis (1993) suggests that it is optimal to work with groups of six to eight children. His experience, following a school sniper attack, was that it was better to run separate groups for boys and girls because of the different reactions they had to the attack. Boys showed more externalising problems and girls showed more internalising ones.

Different authors have imposed varying structures on their groups, with Galante and Foa (1986) adopting an approach where different topics were tackled at each meeting, while Yule and Williams (1990) describe not only an unstructured, problem-solving approach but also ran a parallel group for the parents. Different incidents will require different approaches.

Group approaches seem to be very therapeutic for many children but not all problems can be solved in the group. Gillis (1993) suggests that high risk children – those whose lives were directly threatened, who witnessed death, who were physically injured, who had pre-existing problems or who lack family support, should be offered individual help. More generally, children whose problems persist despite group help should be treated individually.

Individual treatment To date, there is little evidence that drug treatments have a central role, so the focus has been mainly on cognitive behavioural treatments that aim both to help the survivor make sense of what happened and to master feelings of anxiety and helplessness.

Asking children to draw their experience often assists recall of both the event and the emotions (Blom, 1982; Newman, 1976; Galante and Foa, 1986; Pynoos and Eth, 1986). Drawings were not used as 'projective' techniques, but as ways of assisting talking about the experience.

Most survivors recognise that sooner or later 'they must face up to the traumatic event'. The problem for the therapist is how to help the survivor re-experience the event and the emotions that it engenders in such a way that the distress can be controlled rather than magnified. Therapeutic exposure sessions that are too brief may sensitise rather than desensitise (Rachman, 1980) so therapy may require much longer exposure sessions than normal (Saigh, 1986). Useful techniques to promote emotional processing are given elsewhere (Rachman, 1980; Yule 1991; Richards and Lovell, 1990; Richards and Rose, 1991; Saigh, 1992).

Exposure under supportive circumstances seems to deal well with both intrusive thoughts and behavioural avoidance. The other major symptom of child PTSD that requires attention is sleep disorder. A careful analysis will reveal whether the problem is mainly one of getting off to sleep or in waking because of intrusive nightmares related to the disaster. In the former case, implementing relaxing routines before bed and masking thoughts with music may help. In the latter, there are now some promising cognitive behavioural techniques for alleviating nightmares (Palace and Johnston, 1989; Marks, 1978; Halliday, 1987; Seligman and Yellen, 1987).

Ayalon (1983) suggests the use of stress-inoculation techniques (Meichenbaum, 1975, 1977; Meichenbaum and Cameron, 1983), among many others, to prepare Israeli children to cope with the effects of terrorist attacks. These ideas seem eminently sensible, but their implementation awaits systematic evaluation.

The role of schools in helping refugee children

Many schools will already have developed contingency plans to deal with the sort of disasters, large and small, which may hit their community each year. Children may be hurt or killed when travelling to and from school or even when on a school journey; a classroom may be destroyed by arson; an intruder may threaten the lives of children; a teacher may die in front of a class. The school needs to plan ahead not only to decide on how to mobilise resources to deal with a disaster after it hits but also to consider what preventive techniques should be implemented. As far as children are concerned, schools are the most obvious focus for such preventive work.

This is recognised by a number of authors (Johnson, 1993; Yule and Gold, 1993; Klingman, 1993). Not only can schools plan how they will deal with a variety of predictable events – they can consider how to deal with related events in the school curriculum. Thus, an actual crisis should not be the first time that teachers and pupils have discussed death and its surrounding rituals. Schools need to be aware of the variety of faiths practised by pupils and their families so that they know which faiths welcome children at funerals and which do not.

Some consideration might be given to providing children with an introduction to simple stress management techniques which can be augmented when a disaster does strike. Whatever the senior management team may have agreed, schools in which such issues have been discussed will be in a better position than others to help refugee children who may face them with a variety of challenges.

The particular needs of refugee children

So far, the discussion has focused on stress reactions in children with only passing acknowledgement that refugees will probably have experienced an unusual number or degree of stressful experiences. Some people may well protest that it is 'pathologising' or 'medicalising' these experiences to be talking about stress reactions at all, let alone talking about PTSD. It has already been noted that there are wide individual differences in response to stress and by no means all children exposed to a life threatening experience go on to develop PTSD. But many do show other stress reactions and, of course, children who have been uprooted from their homes and who may have lost a parent or other loved one during the turmoil may also have unresolved grief reactions. While recognising that most of these reactions are 'normal' in the sense of being understandable, they still require that action be taken by those in authority to alleviate the children's distress. Diagnosis and labelling are only means to mobilising the needed resources.

It is also true that children can be resilient. As noted earlier, half the adolescents who survived the sinking of the cruise ship, *Jupiter*, went on to develop a full-blown PTSD. Among the others, many showed a number of stress symptoms that interfered with daily life but fell short of a diagnosable condition. While it is true that from the point of view of understanding development it is good to focus more on invulnerable and resilient children, it remains the case that vulnerable ones require help. These stress reactions are not merely transient phenomena that settle down quickly once a child feels safe and secure. That may happen, but in the case of children exposed to war, the long term effects can continue for many years (Elbedour, Bensel and Bastien, 1993). Even in the case of civilian disasters, the effects can be long lasting, so that the seven year follow-up of survivors of the Jupiter sinking is currently reporting that half those who had PTSD within the first year still have it seven years later. Many others experienced other anxiety states and depression in the interim.

So what can and should schools do? The first thing is to note that refugee children are at a higher risk of having mental health problems. It follows, therefore, that the school should ensure that proper monitoring procedures are in force to ensure that help is given when required. This may mean having consultations and discussions with local child guidance, school psychological services and other mental health services, as well as contact with appropriate refugee advocacy groups.

The best thing the school can do is to provide a secure and predictable environment in which the child can settle and learn. Education is highly prized among many refugees as leading to skills that can be taken with the child whatever the outcome of applications for citizenship. Within the pastoral care system, those teachers who will be caring for the refugee need to be alerted to some of the issues discussed above. They need to develop good, trusting relationships with the child in the hope that worries and concerns may be shared.

But this is where a particular problem in working with refugees comes to the fore. As van der Veer (1992) points out, many refugees will have gone to great lengths to escape the country where they felt threatened and may have been involved in illegal activities to get to their country of refuge. They may be suspicious of all people in authority and adults may have told children never to tell outsiders anything. They may have to conceal things they did while fleeing. Until decisions are taken about their future legal status, they will be reticent to share all the truth. Thus, teachers and other adults should not expect children to be totally frank about what happened to them, and this may hinder the process of helping children come to terms with their experiences.

A further complication arises when the fate of those left behind is unclear. Adults try to protect children from the worst, and this may be counterproductive. Discussing the needs of refugee children in Slovenia, a number of teachers told me that the worst thing they had to deal with was when they knew that a child's father had been killed in the war in Bosnia, but the mother had forbidden them to tell the child. A brief discussion confirmed that the teachers agreed that it was by far the best policy to be honest with the children as otherwise when they did discover that the father was dead, they would be angry with mother and teacher and find it harder to trust adults in the future. In any case, the child surely had a right to grieve. In that instance, what started out as a series of crises could be resolved by developing a school policy of openness. Parents would be told that the school would help them to tell children any bad news and would be on hand to support them through the difficult time. Again, teachers helping refugee children need to be aware of any family left behind, who are seen as being at risk from the authorities and need to allow children to share their worries as far as is possible.

In the early days when a child joins a school, the help of an interpreter may be necessary. Here, a further possible complication may have to be considered. Many modern conflagrations are civil wars, often of complex natures and divided along religious or ethnic lines. It is vital to check that any interpreter that one involves is acceptable to the child and family. Families are understandably nervous that emigrés of different groupings may be spies or may feed information back to their original country. Considerable sensitivity is required. To say to a child, 'Oh, you are from Iran [or Iraq, or Rwanda or Bosnia], come and meet another child from there....' without knowing that both children are from compatible subgroups, may be less than helpful! (Issues to do with interpreters are more fully discussed by Van der Veer (1995).

Refugee children will probably have experienced stresses that most of us hope never to face. Many of them will cope reasonably well. Others will cope better if their mental health needs are recognised and appropriate help offered. Schools are in a vital position to ensure that such help is offered. Both in the provision of a good caring atmosphere and in seeking appropriate outside support, schools can make an enormous difference to the future adjustment of children who have been the unwitting victims of adults' failures to resolve differences other than by force.

CHAPTER SIX

Supporting Refugee Children in the Early Years

Tina Hyder

Introduction

I remember when R first started at the playgroup. He was just three and had arrived recently from Eritrea. He was so angry and frustrated he threw things around and hit other children.

Over the weeks he began to trust us and start communicating with the other children. I think he really benefited from his time with us. We were a place of safety.

When S, a four-year-old Kurdish child from Turkey arrived, she also wouldn't communicate, wouldn't play, and for many weeks refused to be physically separated from her mother. It took a long time before she felt able to join in with activities and begin to work out some of her anxieties through play. (Refugee playgroup worker, North London, quoted in Hyder, 1996.)

These snapshots illustrate both the challenge and the importance of early years work with refugee children. Early years workers will increasingly come across children from refugee and asylum-seeking families[1], especially in the inner city. Proportionately there are more under-fives among refugees than other groups, and refugees are more likely to be in need of day-care services (Rutter, 1994). Consequently, effective early years provision can make an important contribution to the lives of young children from asylum-seeking and refugee families. Those with responsibility for planning services must also ensure that services are geared to meet their needs.

Although in some cases specialist support is necessary, the experience of practitioners who work with refugees is increasingly that a period of time in a high-quality mainstream early years setting has made a difference to children – as well as helping to break down the isolation many families face and enabling child and carer to find welcome in a supportive environment.

Refugees are not a homogeneous group: children may be recent arrivals, in temporary accommodation, waiting for the results of asylum applications. They may live with relatives or foster carers, separated from their immediate family. Some children will have been born in this country to parents recently arrived. Others will be members of longer-established refugee communities, such as the Vietnamese community. In some communities, a high percentage of refugee families are headed by women, as men are often victims of conflict from which the rest of a family escapes.

Refugee children will often have experienced conflict and trauma, made worse perhaps by the hardships of life in a refugee camp and the journey from their homeland. They may have witnessed or experienced acts of violence and may not know whether family members are alive or dead. They will certainly have lost the familiar and safe context of childhood and may have been subject to racial harassment or abuse. In this country refugee families may be without possessions or means of support, unable to speak English. There will be feelings of disconnection and isolation, of not belonging. Adults will themselves be stressed, less able to give full attention to the needs of children.

Working with young refugee children therefore poses a complex set of challenges but there are elements of good practice that are applicable in any early years setting. Equal opportunities and anti-racist practices, coupled with good working relationships with parents and carers, recognising and acknowledging family values, are particularly important. Early years practitioners must make efforts to get to know a child and her family, be aware of the many ways children communicate, be effective communicators themselves and be able to support the child as an individual. Crucially, the early years ethos of development through supportive play has particular value for all children. In addition, it is a means to provide the consistent and stimulating environment which is so important for young children from refugee families (Kendrick et al, 1992).

Good practice

An illustrative case study is of value here. A four-year-old Somali boy at a council under-fives centre in London refused to participate in activities or co-operate with staff or other children. Staff were increasingly concerned at his disruptive behaviour. They decided that, rather than continue to ignore his behaviour, an approach that was clearly not working, his key worker would give him at least ten minutes individual attention each day. It quickly became clear that the new strategy was effective, with the boy more able to join in group activities – but also that this was not a short-term intervention. The individual sessions continued for five months, over which period it emerged that the boy had witnessed the shooting of his father. With the support of dedicated, sensitive staff he was able to begin to come to terms with the experience.

Aggressive or disruptive behaviour patterns are just one expression of distress. Naomi Richman, a child psychiatrist who has worked extensively with refugee children for Save the Children, provides a useful guide to the various ways children may manifest feelings about loss, change and separation:

* fear of loud noises or voices, or of groups of men, or men in uniform

* sadness or irritability, children who feel safe will want to engage and play. Distressed children may appear worried, miserable or lacking in energy

* poor concentration and restlessness. children may be 'over-active', unable to settle at any one activity and generally 'silly'

* aggression and disruptiveness – one of the commonest manifestations of distress as well as one of the hardest to deal with. Children may hit out in the absence of other ways of expressing their frustration, may act out inappropriate aggressive behaviour they may have witnessed or may try to keep away from adults or alternatively cling to them, terrified of abandonment

- physical symptoms, such as nightmares, aches and pains, loss of appetite

- frustration and insecurity as a result of unfamiliarity with toys and books, routine, food and customs in the setting. (Derived from Richman, 1993a; 1998).

What can you do? In general it is important to create an atmosphere which is welcoming, safe and reassuring, where the child feels recognised and valued. Some points of good practice:

- ensure the nursery worker is clear about the naming system the family uses and that names are pronounced correctly. This is an important part of reinforcing identity (Zealey, 1995)

- make sure that refugee children and families know the name of the child's key worker. This helps a child, especially when settling in, feel that there is someone who has a special interest in her

- try to build up a profile of the child, so that early years workers know about siblings and extended family, about the child's preferences and dislikes, about family languages and medical history. It may take some time for a family to feel comfortable about giving more than minimal information

- ensure that there is familiar writing and script on welcome posters and notices

- give children an opportunity to hear their family language(s): use tapes of songs and stories in appropriate community languages, and books in dual language form such as the popular *The Very Hungry Caterpillar*

- if children have meals at the nursery, ensure that food from the child's country of origin is sometimes on the menu. This will help children feel comfortable as well as being informative for other children. Parents may be able to help with recipes or advice about buying ingredients. Remember that the use of knives and forks is by no means universal

- posters and pictures of members of the child's community or country of origin, with a mixture of rural and urban images, can also help. Pictures featuring members of the community participating in everyday British life as well, will add to children's sense that there is a place for them in their new country. Remember to bear in mind differences between refugee groups from the same country (Refugee Council, 1994b).

Feelings

Again, an illustrative case study is useful to frame the discussion. At the Save the Children's Deptford Family Resource Centre, a brother and sister dived under the table every time they heard loud noises or planes overhead. They had recently arrived from a refugee camp. Staff discovered that this was because of an incident when the family were under attack, and to reduce this fear devised a series of activities around the theme of 'feelings', using stories, puppet shows, music, dance and discussion as well as painting, model-making and imaginative play. Without introducing specific information about being pursued or shot at, or about bombs or shelling, which might have been distressing, the opportunity was offered to talk in small groups about 'what scares me', 'what makes me happy', 'what do I feel like if someone shouts at me or calls me names'.

By sharing concrete examples and experiences and being together with supportive adults, the children were able to empathise and to understand that everyone gets scared, and that expressing fear is understandable and acceptable. The children were able to offer each other support, and share creative ideas about dealing with real or imagined fears.

All young children experience strong emotions and refugee children may have lived through particularly traumatic events. In general, children start to use words to describe their feelings from before the age of two. Between two and three there is a rapid increase in the number of terms children are able to use in describing different emotions; as they get older they learn to label emotions correctly and to use emotional language in pretend play. From four onwards they understand that the same event may generate different emotions in different people, and that feelings may persist long after the event itself is past (Kuebli, 1994).

Research also suggests that children's early understanding of some emotional situations may considerably outpace their ability to express their feelings or understanding in words. Children will communicate their feelings in many ways, verbally and non-verbally. Workers may not share a child's home language and children may be too traumatised to speak but it remains important to communicate, perhaps by using body language.

Workers can create opportunities for play, where refugee children can feel all-powerful, or magic, or invisible. Pretend play such as this offers a way for all children and particularly refugee children to begin to make sense of how they feel and come to terms with past experiences. Dramatic play, including mime and mask-making, pretending, imaginative sessions with miniature figures, painting and drawing all offer children ways to express their feelings which workers should encourage and support.

Language and communication
Refugee children may well speak two or more languages other than English and early years settings offer a rich learning environment where children can develop their language skills. Supporting a child's first language(s) both enhances their ability to learn English and increases their self-esteem and confidence in their own ethnicity. Research has shown that children with a solid foundation in their first language are able to transfer skills when learning a second language and there are well-documented stages of such additional language acquisition (Edwards, 1995).

In particular, children in the early stages may say little or nothing in the new language – but they will be observing others and gaining the confidence they need to start communication. There will be considerable variation between learners, and before learning can take place children need to feel secure. It is important to be familiar with these behaviours and not confuse them with developmental delay or signs of trauma or distress.

Miller (1992) suggests useful guidelines to encourage language development:

- build trust through eye contact, smiles and making time for the child

- learn key words in the child's first language, particularly greetings and forms of address. Find out from parents how children will tell you when they need to go to the bathroom, when they are hungry and so on

- be a good language model yourself, speaking slowly but in a normal voice

- remember that children can understand what is said long before they can express themselves in the new language. It is important that their environment is language-rich

- encourage productive language – hello and goodbye. Make efforts to understand non-verbal communication and fill in the words

- encourage interaction between children. Let children teach you and the other children some words in their home language, while others in the group can be guides and 'buddies' to the non-English speakers

- encourage families to have contact with the centre, coming in to cook, tell a story or read a book in their home language.

Culture, identity and valuing diversity

Maintenance of cultural links and identity is important to all children . Refugee children need to be grounded in their first language and culture, to see being Somali, Kurdish or Vietnamese, for example, as something to be proud of. Cultural identity is typically established by the age of five and for people operating, as refugees are, in more than one culture, there are three important aspects of 'cross-cultural competence':

- self-awareness

- knowledge of information specific to each culture

- skills which enable the individual to engage in each culture (Hanson and Lynch, 1992).

It is important that people working with children from minority ethnic and refugee communities are aware of the different ways that behaviour is culturally based. The importance attached to privacy and indivi-duality is not universal. Body language is culturally determined, as are attitudes to young children's behaviour – whether talking back and interrupting is seen as misbehaviour or to be encouraged.

At the same time assumptions should not be made. There are wide variations within cultures, and many factors – socio-economic, religious, regional – can influence behaviour. It is important for early years workers to learn about the cultures and the communities of the families they are working with by reading, talking and working with individuals from particular communities, participating where possible in the everyday life of the community or by learning some of the languages of the communities worked with.

Research has shown that children as young as two or three years old are aware of difference and begin to develop positive and negative feelings about difference. It is important that early years workers support all children to notice similarities and differences in the way children and adults look, speak and dress in their family groups and to see difference as positive. Unless work is done by early years educators on valuing diversity from the start, children will absorb the implicit and explicit messages about what is supposed to be 'normal' in society (Sparks, 1989).

Children from refugee and asylum seeking families need to see resources that reflect a range of family groups. For example, a mother and her children, or children living with their grandparents. Children also need to hear stories and songs from their family's country of origin, seeing other children enjoy translated folk tales, or dancing to music that is a family favourite will make children feel that they are accepted, have something to offer and that home is not something to be ashamed of. As part of this process, books, posters, puzzles, games and toys must be evaluated for messages about diversity to ensure they contain positive, realistic and accurate images that are not stereotyped or exotic.

Home corners are a vital and adaptable part of any early years setting. As well as reflecting a variety of homes, home corners can be transformed into airports, hospitals or launderettes, and offer opportunities for children to act out situations they have experienced (for example arriving in the UK at the airport) and/or are currently experiencing that are new and strange (for example using a launderette). In addition, they also can reflect the way things are done at home (Clarke and Millikan, 1986). Many settings already use a range of cooking and eating utensils such as chopsticks and pots to make tea. Other props are also useful. Model food can be made from clay or playdough or bought from educational suppliers: all offer a useful starting point for staff and children. There are many other examples. A range of realistic looking plastic breads from around the world present early years workers with the basis of an exciting theme and are important additions to the home corner. Models of injera from Ethiopia and Chinese steamed buns as well as rye, white and whole-wheat bread provide opportunities for children to say to each other 'my family eats this'. Making the real thing is the next step, and this provides children with the chance to smell, taste and be involved in food preparation as happens at home.

Home corners without the usual miniature tables and chairs offer children the chance to sit on the floor or on low stools and to take tea, eat and talk as they have seen their parents and grandparents do. Home corners can be hung with inexpensive decorative cloth that is familiar and attractive, while a wide range of dressing-up clothes can be provided with a stress on everyday clothes from a range of communities . It is important that dressing-up clothes are not just exotic, but represent a realistic representation of styles from different communities as well as allowing children a way to take on roles and develop imaginative play skills. Clothes can be bought from suppliers or made, a role that may offer refugee parents a chance to get involved.

Music and dance are also enjoyed by all children and offer opportunities for expression regardless of language skills. Very young children below the age of two can be seen to respond to music that is part of the home environment. A collection of music from different countries will reassure children particularly when they are settling in to the centre. A wide range of instruments allow children to experiment and play.

The global curriculum

Children's ideas about themselves and the world around them are formed at an early age. They take note of what is going on in their own place, their own family and in places further away. As they grow up, children's ideas often become more fixed and stereotypes develop. By introducing young children to the wealth of traditions, ways of doing things, ranges of lifestyles in our world, we can play an active part in influencing how young children see the world (Education Development Centre, 1996).

It is possible to work with young children to broaden their knowledge of the world, and so bring a global perspective to early years work. In this way, the stories of refugee children in the early years setting can be included. Themes such as 'journeys' take a child's experiences as the starting point. The journey be long or as short, from Zaire to Heathrow or from the top of the road to nursery. It is also possible to find photographs and images that give children an idea of life outside and UK from newspapers and magazines, from museums and charities, aid agencies and multicultural bookshops; early years workers can take photographs of children; families may supply others. These images can be used in displays or in a range of activities. An activity might involve children sorting pictures of all the different types of home and house they have from around the world. Photographs where people are always poor or in difficulty should be avoided, and it is important to try and keep a balance of rural and urban scenes. A world map with pictures of children showing where they and their parents have come from is a good start.

Wider issues

Again, a case study helps frame the subsequent discussion. The Deptford Vietnamese Health Project was established to identify the health needs of the local Vietnamese community, and particularly to look at ways of joint working between agencies. Supported jointly by Save the Children and the local health authority, it worked closely with Save the Children's Deptford Family Resource Centre, which provides day-care for refugee and other children. A number of issues around childcare and children's health were identified. In one case a three-year-olds' difficulties in talking and understanding had been ascribed after a developmental check to his lack of English. Close liaison between his mother, the health project and the resource centre revealed other circumstances, including previous physical abuse. The project has revealed the value of co-ordination between agencies and the importance of outreach and appropriate communication, in this case through employing Vietnamese staff.

This project has demonstrated the importance of working closely with parents. This should not be limited to parents of children using the establishment. Services need to find out about the groups of refugee families settled in their area and do outreach work. Barriers to use of early years services are numerous, beginning with the fact that many refugee families simply do not know what services are available, as much research has shown. Translated material alone may not reach families effectively, particularly where men and women may not be literate in their home language.

The Islington playgroup mentioned at the beginning of this chapter was set up when it was recognised that, despite the large number of refugee families in the borough, only 13 children from refugee or asylum seeking families were attending council day-care. Users of the playgroup have included Turkish, Kurdish, Somali and Eritrean families, with obvious benefits for children and parents.

Fees and charges may put places beyond the means of refugee parents, and isolated carers may feel too scared to use early years services because of the distance they have to walk with younger children or because of fear of harassment. It may be possible to prioritise places for children from refugee families. The benefits even of a place for only a few weeks until the end of term have been noted by workers. Local authorities and voluntary organisations need to ensure that parents and carers know that there are places in playgroups and nurseries for their children. This may mean translating written material into relevant languages, contacting refugee community groups and hostels to let families know what's available, and using community radio. Outreach work may also require visits to community centres and bed and breakfast hostels by people who can explain directly what is available where parents are not literate either in English or their home language.

It may be the case that, traditionally, young children are cared for at home within the extended family, indicating a need for recruitment of childminders from the particular community, alongside appropriate support. Or there may be no-one in the setting with appropriate language skills and knowledge of the community's child-rearing practices. Toilet training can be a difficult issue, for example. Training via nappies and potty, alongside western taboos about bodily functions and control, is very different from practices in many communities.

Refugee families may place enormous importance on education. The value of play as a means of discovery and vital foundation for the acquisition of learning skills may need to be emphasised if parents see early years settings as missing opportunities for children to begin formal education in literacy and numeracy.

In times of stress, customs and tradition may well be more important in maintaining the fabric of family life. Early years workers must be flexible and ensure that provision reflects, within day-to-day practice, the experiences of children within the home, and allows children to feel continuity and acceptance between home and the early years setting.

The provision of high-quality, appropriate early years services is only a part of the wider support required by refugee families, as recent research by the Daycare Trust has shown (Sherriff, 1995). The trust's First Base project combined in-depth research with refugee families from the Horn of Africa, pilot training programmes in childcare for refugee women, and the gathering of good practice guidelines via surveys across the country designed to identify the characteristics of services best meeting the needs of refugee children. The research report sets out a comprehensive agenda for early years services and policy-makers, derived from the views of parents and refugee community organisations nation-wide. Its four main conclusions were:

1. For parents, it identified a need not only for high quality childcare but also additional English language support and wider services, along the lines of those developed in family centres, particularly aimed at bringing together childcare, training and welfare support.

2. Agencies and statutory bodies need to develop better understanding of refugees, and combine multicultural approaches with practi-

cal support – education and training opportunities backed up with childcare and financial assistance.

3. Effective communication – via outreach in appropriate languages – is vital, and local authorities and other agencies need to collect accurate data, review the use made by refugee families of pre-school education, care and other services, and set targets to improve take-up.

4. There should also be support for refugee community organisations, and greater efforts to employ members of refugee communities and take students on placement.

On a wider scale, and based partly on research overseas, particularly in Holland, the report suggests that a national policy towards assisting refugees should be developed by central government, under the auspices of a single department. The policy should cover research into education, childcare, social services, health, employment, adult education and training. Without such a national lead, it is unlikely the complete range of educational needs of young refugee children will be adequately met in the foreseeable future.

Thanks to Jill Redshaw and Charles Wright for their comments on the chapter.

Note

1. Refugee families will have varying legal staus; the term 'refugee' is used throughout this chapter as a generic term rather than as a legal definition. Similarly, the terms 'parent(s) are used throughout to designate primary carers who may or may not be the biological parents.

CHAPTER SEVEN

Supporting Refugee Children in East London Primary Schools

Bill Bolloten and Tim Spafford

Introduction

In this chapter we describe our work as Refugee Support Teachers and look at some of the key issues facing teachers of refugee children in the London Borough of Newham. We consider some of the recent research that raises awareness about the experiences of refugees, and draw on case studies of refugee children we have worked with, to suggest good practice.

The role of the Refugee Support Teacher

Refugees coming to a British school for the first time may have escaped recently from persecution and organised violence. They are unlikely to have had any formal welcome on their arrival in this country or the borough they are housed in. Before arriving in school, refugee families experience many obstacles in their attempts to secure food, warmth and shelter. This is becoming more arduous in the present climate of growing disbelief or outright hostility to refugees and asylum seekers.

As Refugee Support Teachers we aim therefore to help children feel safe when they start school. We extend a welcome also to their parents and carers, being aware that children's wider needs may not be understood or responded to. In schools we identify need through observation and consultation and build partnerships with class teachers in planning, resourcing and delivering lessons. We also support schools in developing a whole-school approach to the needs of refugee pupils, co-ordinating multi-agency work with families and liaising with refugee community organisations. Finally, we provide INSET to teachers and other professionals working in schools.

Refugee Communities in Newham

The most recent estimates indicate that there may be more than 15,000 refugees and asylum seekers living in the London Borough of Newham (Bloch, 1994). In 1997 there were more than 3,500 refugee children enrolled in local schools. Refugee children currently form around 8 per cent of the total school roll. The Benefits Agency has identified over 10,000 'persons from abroad' who live in Newham and who are on reduced benefit levels while they await decisions from the Home Office on their asylum claims. With 81 per cent of all Home Office decisions on asylum applications now being refusals, many refugees in Newham are facing a future of uncertainty and insecurity.

The largest refugee communities in Newham are from Somalia and Sri Lanka. There are also significant numbers from Zaire, Angola, Uganda, Eritrea, Ethiopia, Vietnam, Turkey, Nigeria and Kenya. Around 30 unaccompanied refugee children are cared for by Social Services. As in London as a whole, many refugees in Newham are homeless and are living in temporary accommodation. This includes housing in the private sector on a short – term lease basis, and bed and breakfast hotels. Much of the accommodation is overcrowded and unsuitable for families with children. The effects on the education of children living in temporary accommodation are well documented (Shelter, 1995).

Many schools in Newham face pressures in settling refugee children who arrive as 'unplanned' admissions during the school term. Some of these children are newly-arrived in Britain; others have moved home many times due to their parents and carers having no access to per-manent accommodation. As high numbers of children in the borough change schools frequently their academic progress is disrupted and friendships they have made are often lost. The experience of one Kurdish refugee child is not untypical

I've been in six schools in four years and lived in five different houses. My brother used to cry because it was hard for him to get used to each new school (Baily, 1995).

Understanding the refugee experience

Teachers may sometimes show a reluctance to develop an understanding of the experiences of refugees. Fear of being overwhelmed by the complexity of their situation, their needs and their anxieties, may cause some professionals to withdraw or distance themselves. This was confirmed by the findings of a research project by the Daycare Trust (Sherriff, 1995). Parents from Somalia and Eritrea remarked that professionals in health, social services and education had little understanding of the difference between refugees and migrants and were therefore unlikely to take into account the effects of being a refugee. The parents also felt that professionals had little understanding of their culture, background and lifestyles.

Raising awareness of what it means to be a refugee and making available information on the particular backgrounds of refugee communities is a vital first step in understanding the needs of refugee children. While stressing that refugees have very diverse backgrounds and are unique individuals with different experiences of persecution, flight and exile, the refugee experience is, as Ron Baker has written, essentially one that involves loss.

Loss of what is obvious, tangible and external such as possessions, a home, work, role, status, life style, a language, loved members of the family or other close relationships; and loss that is less obvious, 'internal' and 'subjective' such as loss of trust in the self and others, loss of self esteem, self respect and personal identity (Baker, 1983).

Ron Baker constructed a simple diagram, which he called a 'relationship web', which is helpful in understanding the position of a refugee. A person is normally held in position in his or her culture by a 'web' of relationships and connections to other people and social structures. These provide status, affirmation and a sense of connection and belonging. (See Diagram 7.1)

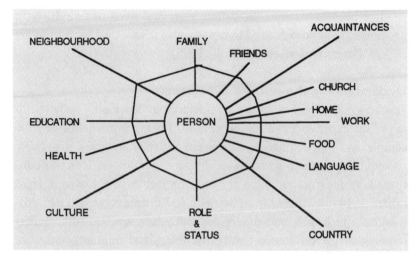

Diagram 7.1: the 'web' of relationships and connections to other people and social structures.

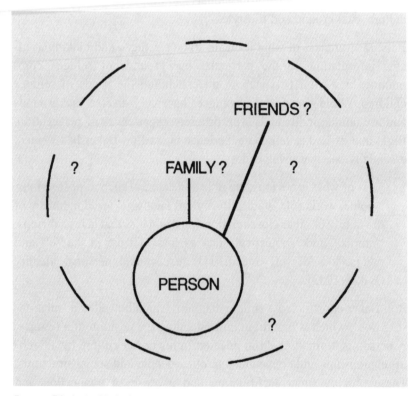

Diagram 7.2: the 'web' of relationships and connections to other people and social structures of many refugees

In the process of being forcibly uprooted and becoming a refugee, a person is 'usually dramatically stripped of this web... (representing)... a massive threat and challenge to the individual's coping and adaptive capacities' (Ibid.). (See Diagram 7.2)

The 'relationship web' is a model of some value because it shows us the extent of the loss occurring from a fracturing of relationship networks. It can suggest some of the interventions and strategies that a school may adopt to support refugee children. Ron Baker himself argues that 'help will be or ought to be directed toward rebuilding (the) relationship web in a variety of ways' (Ibid.).

An assumption frequently made by schools is that refugee children who have been exposed to armed conflict and human rights abuses, will be 'traumatised'. It may be tempting to form this conclusion when children start school and display behaviour that causes concern. In fact the experience of many schools suggests that while some children do indeed show acute distress and appear unable to manage their experiences and move on, many other refugee children cope and function well in the classroom, make stable friendships and progress in their learning.

Research suggests that children who have endured persecution, political violence and exile will have been subjected to a range of stressors. Alongside these are mediating factors which may offer protection against trauma and distress and which can help to explain the variety of coping behaviours and strategies that teachers observe in children. If schools can be aware that these processes exist and interrelate, more informed assessments can be made of a child's situation and planning can proceed that responds to the needs of the whole child.

In the ecological framework proposed by Elbadour, ten Bensel and Bastien (1993), five key mediating factors have been identified as influencing the coping capacity of a child. Understanding the presence of these factors will automatically raise questions about practice in schools.

Firstly, the inner psychological resources and developmental characteristics of each *individual* child, along with factors such as their age and gender will influence whether a child will experience detrimental emotional outcomes to his or her experiences. This raises questions such as:

- *In what ways can schools consider a child's developmental history?*

- *What events and losses has a child experienced and when?*

Secondly, research suggests that a child's *family* can act as a protective shield, mitigating some of the effects of stress and trauma. 'Parents who deal with trauma will tend to pass on positive mental health to their children; those who cope poorly tend to pass on their stress' (Ibid.). Schools are often unaware of the extent to which a child's ties to family have been broken – both by events in their country of origin and by difficulties gaining a family reunion under the present immigration rules in the UK.

- *How can schools themselves, or in partnership with other services, give support to a child's family?*

Links to a wider *community* are vital for all of us. For refugee children, who may have lost the support of immediate family members, the embrace of a community can help to rebuild a sense of belonging and reduce the stress of isolation. The ethos and values of a school community can also be crucial in reassuring children of their safety.

- *How can schools extend a sense of safety and stability to all pupils?*

- *When schools are often the only public neighbourhood facility, can they provide space for refugee parents and communities to meet together?*

A child's *culture*, ideology and political or religious beliefs can also shape the way experiences are dealt with. When your community and its cultural identity have been subjected to repression, or even outlawed, contact with people who share your language, culture and background can support children in regaining a sense of order and belonging.

- *In what ways can schools inform themselves of the cultural back-grounds of refugee families?*

- *Does the school ethos and curriculum affirm their presence?*

Finally, the *intensity, duration and suddenness of conflict* will affect how a child copes. Some children may become used to dangers and anxieties after living for years in zones of conflict and unrest, and may even view the situation as 'normal'. Other children, however, may have experienced a sudden and unexpected outbreak of violence.

- *How can schools ensure that all children feel safe?*

- *In what ways can teachers show empathy with the unique situation of each child?*

The role of the school

The ecological model has clear implications for practice. By under-standing that refugee children, along with their families and communities, have wider needs, schools can ensure that support is focused in a systematic way through communication, liaison and co-ordination with other services. Primary schools are particularly well resourced by their day-to-day contact with parents and carers. The development of the community role that schools can play has recently been strongly supported in recommendations prepared for Manchester City Council by the National Children's Bureau (Klein, 1995). In this model, education, health and social services will be brought together into comprehensive and integrated children's support services, based *in* the city's schools.

In Newham we have sought to respond to the needs of refugee children by supporting and extending good practice in five key areas. These are:

- ensuring that children have access to the school curriculum

- recognising and validating children's experiences

- helping children cope with separation and loss

- building home – school partnerships and

- giving advice and support to teachers and other professionals.

Each of these is now looked at in more detail.

Access to the school curriculum Those who have fled to Britain now face unprecedented obstacles in securing asylum. The withdrawal of welfare benefits from the majority of asylum-seekers, coupled with measures in the Asylum and Immigration Act 1996, will compound their insecurity. While at present schools are not required to check the immigration status of new children, a consequence of the new legislation will be to create anxiety and undermine the trusting relationships that many schools have built with refugee parents. There is also evidence that many refugee parents are finding it increasingly difficult to find school places for their children.

It is important to reaffirm that local education authorities have a legal responsibility to provide schooling to refugee and asylum-seeking children. In schools, refugee children have the right of access to the whole school curriculum. We must restate our commitment to an ethos that is inclusive of refugees, that values their language abilities, their skills and experiences, and their contribution to school life.

Schools must address the needs of bilingual refugee learners in their planning for the language and pastoral needs of all pupils. In Newham, recently published borough *Guidelines on Whole – School Language Policies and Bilingual English Learners* (Newham, 1996) asks schools to consider as key principles that:

- Bilingual learners acquire English language skills most effectively by working alongside their English-speaking peers, as they develop social relations with them

- Lack of English should not be equated with lack of ability. Both pupils and teachers should have high expectations of bilingual learners. This has clear implications for setting and streaming arrangements where they exist.

Clearly there are also implications for resourcing schools with appropriate books and materials. Schools are not always aware that there are such resources available, mostly from smaller publishing houses. Dual language and mother tongue books give status to the linguistic heritage of refugee children and can be used successfully in providing opportunities for parents to read at home. The increasing range of dual language editions marketed by Mantra Publishing now includes many books already in regular use in primary classrooms, such as The Very Hungry Caterpillar. Mantra are also developing a range of simple dictionaries for primary children in languages that include Somali, Arabic, Turkish and French.

HAAN Associates, a Somali community publishing venture, has produced a variety of materials for schools, including dual language phrase books and subject dictionaries, information booklets about Somali history and culture, stories and a Somali colouring book.

Some local education authorities have also developed materials in the languages of refugee communities. The Enfield Language and Curriculum Access Service has translated an extensive range of popular primary texts into Turkish and Somali. Learning Design in Tower Hamlets has published dual language editions of Kurdish and Somali folk tales, making the rich oral tradition of these languages available to new audiences. Brent Travellers and Displaced Persons Education Service have published a Somali Language Pack. Aimed at primary and secondary children it contains useful phrases, vocabulary guides and some classroom activities for newly arrived pupils.

Books that help young children to understand about the experiences of refugees also have a place in all mainstream classrooms. *The Don't Forget Us* series (Watts) introduces the history, culture and lifestyles of refugee children from countries including Somalia, Kurdistan, Vietnam and Bosnia. The books use a child's personal narrative and compare life in their homeland with their new life in their adopted country. Save the Children have published a resource pack for 4-7 year olds, *New Faces, New Places*, containing four story booklets about refugees in Africa, Vietnam, Palestine and Kurdistan.

Recognising and validating children's experiences Autobiographical writing and life story work can help children to understand their often fragmented personal histories. Life story work can be approached in many ways with younger pupils. Its importance is often recognised for all children in curriculum work on 'Ourselves'. In a safe and supportive classroom environment, life story work can enable memories to be processed and acknowledged by different audiences.

The *Voices* series published by the Minority Rights Group is another resource that can support children's autobiographical work. The books collect together the drawings and life stories of refugee children and adults from different countries. Many teachers have also found *Talking Time*, published by Learning Design in Tower Hamlets, to be a useful handbook for developing children's oral histories.

Some refugee children will choose to draw pictures of events in their life, sometimes repeating the same images. The therapeutic value of such work was confirmed by research into the effect of endemic violence on pre-school children in South African townships (Magwaza, 1993). Children who expressed their memories and feelings through art were found to be less likely to suffer from Post Traumatic Stress Disorder. Such drawings and paintings, photographs and simple time-lines can all help children make sense of their life histories and begin to build a coherent inner narrative for themselves. As children's literacy improves they can 'revisit' their work and add to their earlier accounts.

Case study

Paul was in a Year Two class at a primary school in London. Paul's family were from Zaire and Paul had been in the UK for less than a year. Sometimes he was not picked up from school and not given any 'tuck money'. The family had been forced to leave Paul's young sister, Agnes, behind in Zaire.

Paul's behaviour at school was at first seemingly bizarre. Teachers found him very difficult to control. However, with regular one-to-one supervision from a General Welfare Assistant, both first thing in the morning and at break times, and through plenty of extra opportunities for supervised play, Paul was able to feel more secure and settled. Although Paul was making good progress in his understanding of spoken English, he easily became frustrated when unable to express himself. He would often stutter with the effort of recalling or finding new words. Paul loved listening to stories read in class and also drew pictures to convey meaning.

In one lesson Paul drew a series of pictures about journeys. Paul's teacher encouraged him to talk about his pictures and gave him lots of encouragement and praise. Paul recalled some of his memories of Zaire.

Paul: Let me show you something. (*Paul collected another picture from his tray. It was a picture of a small person climbing a tree. Paul then drew a soldier by a tree*).

Teacher: OK You jump on the tree...

Paul: Yeah..

Teacher : ...and then what else do you do?

Paul: *(stammering) (inaudible)* ... and then I fall d.. whooaaaaa *(falling down noise)*

Teacher: You fall down?

Paul: Yeah I fall down and then I jump... water is there...and then someone get me ... and then ... *(inaudible)* ... I'm dead.

Teacher: Oh no!

Paul: Some ... he push me ... and then .... he push me .... *(stammer)* ... dead.

Teacher: ... and you're dead?

Paul: Yeah.

Teacher: Can you go to hospital and get better?

Paul: Yeah. I got better...... Som.... he push me he shoota me ... *(made shooting noise)* ... he shoota me.

Teacher: Have you seen soldiers like that?

Paul: Yeah!

Teacher: Did they push you?

Paul: Yeah. They push me.

Paul finished by drawing a flower which he remembered was outside the door of his house. The teacher looked through the drawings. Paul numbered the pictures and agreed to tell the story of all of them.

Paul: Sometime I go in the tree... and someone soldiers and they do get me, they push me and then they push me and then tree...

and I'm dead... I go strong... and then... sometimes I go home
I sleep my bed... and then... (*inaudible*)... when I close my
door I see my... (*inaudible*)... flower... it's lovely flowers.

By drawing pictures and talking about them, Paul was given opportunities to use English meaningfully and by listening and showing an
active interest, the teacher helped Paul share his story and receive
affirmation.

Helping children to cope with separation and loss Both Richman
(1993a) and Melzak and Warner (1992) have acknowledged that although all refugee children need time and space to adjust to loss,
change and displacement, they do not all necessarily need 'specialist'
help. Indeed as Richman remarks:

> Most descriptions of help focus on specific clinical interventions
> but the child's social and material situation must also be addressed.
> The provision of basic material needs, health and education
> services, pre-school and recreational facilities, community centres,
> etc., are essential aspects of help. Many refugee families in Britain
> for example are affected as much by their constricted social life,
> lack of work and recreational possibilities, as by their past
> suffering (Richman, 1993a).

Western models of therapeutic support may not be culturally appropriate for many refugee communities, and, at the present time, demand
for such services exceeds what is available. However, mainstream primary classes are often very successful in supporting the emotional and
social needs of children coming to terms with separation and loss.
Cheerful, affirmative classrooms with a range of enjoyable activities
provide children with normality, structure and daily routines of great
healing potential. The primary curriculum also provides considerable
scope for raising issues of loss and change with all children. Creative
and group activities, including music, play, drama, role-play, art and
storytelling can be vehicles for exploring positive feelings as well as
painful and sad ones.

Teachers who make space for children's feelings to be discussed, will
understand that this can best happen in a class where children feel safe.
Their feelings of sadness, anger and grief can be 'held' by the group,

who can support and other and learn new personal and social skills. Teachers who communicate warmth and acceptance, who are patient and available to listen when a child speaks, will be able to build trusting relationships with refugee children. At times this will challenge us to think and feel about the experiences of children. 'What children can tell us depends, to a large extent, upon what adults are prepared to hear' (Garbarino, 1993).

Case study

Saeed, who was from Somalia, was in a Year Five class. He had been in the UK for more than three years. Saeed and his family had fled from northern Somalia following the outbreak of war there in 1988. They had lived in a refugee camp in Ethiopia for almost three years. Soon after coming to London, Saeed's father left the family. At the same time the family learnt that a much-loved aunt had died of starvation.

The school was concerned that Saeed was not making progress with writing and that he seemed very sad and depressed. He often seemed isolated. Saeed had also been a victim of racist bullying in school.

Saeed's class were working on a topic entitled 'The Communities of London'. The children first role-played a Miroslav Holub poem, The Door, that freed them to explore their own imaginary worlds. Saeed then wrote the following:

Mum walk with me through the wardrobe
it may lead to trouble
it may lead to another world.

We may save the other world from evil spirits,
we may even break the spell by the white witch.

Saeed, almost instinctively, created structure and shape in his writing. He became aware of the other children as an audience for his work. He also shared his poem with his mother. All the children's poems were all displayed in a class booklet for children to borrow. Saeed was keen for his poem to be included in the collection.

Through further autobiographical work, which included drama, the class began to research their family's experiences of war. Saeed found this work difficult, due to his own feelings of sadness and of feeling different because of the extent of his own losses. It was not easy for him. Yet when he found that he could enjoy and begin to explore his relationships with his peers in safety, Saeed gained confidence and started to find the words to describe his own feelings. He approached the teacher as a confidant, expressing his anger, sadness and fears.

Later, Saeed wrote the following:

> Me and my mum, my brothers and sister were in my auntie's house and an aeroplane stopped. We all thought it was going to drop a bomb on us but after a while it went away. My mum hid all her valuables in the ground. Soldiers used to stamp on the ground. If they hit something hard they would dig it up and get it.
>
> Once me and my mum had to change our names and lie about who we were so we could go in a house and have enough to eat and sleep there for the night. That night we had to be disguised. When my mum returned there later it had disappeared.

Saeed's class were able to see a different side to Saeed and valued his good feelings for others. Saeed had found some support despite his fears for his family, his concerns for his mother and his sometimes overwhelming desire to push it all away.

Case study

Rui, an Angolan child, arrived in a primary school and joined a Year Five class. He spoke good Portuguese and made rapid progress with English. A few weeks after settling into school in the UK, Rui began to show aggression towards pupils and teachers, occasionally exploding into a violent rage. The school met and talked with Rui's family and began to learn about his recent experiences .

Rui had joined his parents sometime after they had fled to the UK. Rui and his twin sister had been left behind in Angola, in the care of an adult who was abusive towards them. Rui had witnessed violence perpetrated against his family and had seen the death of a close family member. Rui's twin sister was still in Angola.

Initial responses from the school were conflicting. On the one hand, teachers wanted to help Rui but on the other, they felt overwhelmed by his difficulties. Some teachers felt it would be better to refer him to an off-site behavioural support unit. However, one teacher, who was available to work with Rui, was committed to helping him through his difficulties in the school. This teacher supported a programme designed to help Rui feel safe and able to participate in normal class activities. It included providing safe areas for Rui in the class, time for one-to-one support, monitoring of progress and regular review meetings with his family. These meetings were supported by inter-pretation. School work was to include friendship-building activities in small groups and pairs, creative work, life-story work where possible, access to mother-tongue materials and extra play opportunities. Rui was also welcomed as a 'helper' in the nursery twice a week. In further review meetings with his family, the school provided books for home-reading in Portuguese, discussed the importance of special play and reading time for Rui and encouraged the family's attendance at sessions arranged at the local Child and Family Consultation Service. As a result of all this, Rui's teachers came to recognise the importance of a co-ordinated multi-agency response to his needs, and the central role the school could play in offering protection and therapeutic help.

Building a home – school partnership Much of the good practice we have outlined above takes a partnership between home and school almost for granted. Indeed some current research concludes that parent-teacher partnerships are essential if children are to learn effectively in school (Pollard and Filer, 1996). However, schools who have built up effective partnerships with the home will testify to how much planning and effort it can take. A great deal is determined by how you begin a relationship with carers, and for refugee families who often seek school admission of their children during the school year, the wel-come and involvement they are offered by the school can significantly affect the initial progress of the child, and the capacity of the family to provide help.

There are a variety of ways in which schools can improve their admission and induction of refugee children (see Spafford and Bolloten 1995). Many newly-arriving refugee families are not informed about the English education system, and may not be aware of an age-related curriculum. They may not know about free school meals or school clothing grants. They may also be unaware of their legal requirements to support their child's school attendance.

A short, translated 'welcome leaflet' has been found to be an effective way of giving this information. Families can additionally be informed about school routines, educational visits, parents evenings and the availability of English classes for adults.

Giving advice and support to teachers Teachers and other education professionals working with refugee children need support and under-standing themselves. Their work can place sustained demands on their time, professional skill and their own inner resources. In thinking about the lives of refugee children, teachers will be confronted with some of the realities of the abuses of human rights taking place in the world today. At times they may experience similar feelings of isolation, dis-integration, regression, disconnection, rage and helplessness to those of refugees themselves (Melzak, op. cit.).

As Refugee Support Teachers we have often struggled to contain our feelings of relative powerlessness and our anger at the situation of children and families with whom we work. At the same time we have to provide consistency in our practice. The fragmentation and at times complete absence of other agencies or networks that may help families, often exacerbates such stresses on ourselves and other front line workers.

Good practice in schools would start from an understanding that the welcome and care of refugee children is a whole school responsibility. A school may choose to identify an experienced member of staff to liaise with outside agencies and refugee communities, co-ordinate in-service training and staff development, make available information about refugee communities and ensure a consistent approach is shared by all workers, including ancillary and non-teaching staff. Staff should be briefed about current changes affecting refugee children, such as the withdrawal of welfare benefits.

Finally, school managers need to be aware of the pressures staff sometimes face by themselves being aware of the experiences of their refugee children.

Conclusion

Many schools achieve real success in their work with refugee children. Though they may not feel equipped to meet some of their wider needs, they are learning to value the wealth of understanding they gain from admitting them, and the reaffirmation such connection can give of a school's relationship with the world.

The Asylum and Immigration Act 1996 withdrew benefits from many asylum-seekers and restricted their access to local authority housing. Schools are now facing new pressures. Children will become homeless and will be at risk of malnutrition and ill health. Without the support of schools the consequences for many children will be devastating. Teachers are asking how can their schools help to feed children? How can they help children to continue to attend school when they have no means to pay for travel? What welfare and campaigning initiatives can schools take in partnership with local communities? How can their schools reassure families of their support and show an interest in their struggle against persecution – a struggle that may be continuing here in Britain?

A school's contact with refugees can enhance its awareness of global issues and prompt it into articulating a clear stand against war, violence and the abuse of human rights. It can support a school in developing links with its local community, informing and extending the scope of the curriculum. The more connections all children make with each other's experiences, the more 'normal' will be the refugee child's presence in school.

CHAPTER EIGHT

Working with Refugee Children: One School's Experience

Caroline Lodge

Introduction

This chapter draws on the experience of one mixed secondary school in north London for three purposes:

- to describe the experiences gained from working with refugee children

- to describe what we learned at whole school level, classroom and curriculum level and individual level

- and to draw out some implications and issues from our experience because these may be of use to others.

From 1992 onwards a growing number of refugee children were admitted to George Orwell School in Islington. I was headteacher from 1989-1995. By 1994/5 about a third of our students were of refugee origin, 150 out of 550 students, mainly from Turkish Kurdistan, but also from Somalia, Eritrea, Ethiopia, South America, Sri Lanka and eastern Europe. They came to our school because of a combination of factors: we had spaces, there was a lot of temporary accommodation near the school, and many of them had contacts through other refugee families whose children already attended George Orwell School. The experience of the school was unique only in the concentration and number of children arriving. Many other schools in London found themselves having to respond to the needs of refugee children at this time.

ιd change in the composition of the school roll was only one of ιany changes which the school was managing at the time: we were also coping with the introduction of Local Management of Schools (LMS), adapting our curriculum to include National Curriculum requirements and many other externally imposed changes resulting from the Education Reform Act 1988. The changes in our roll brought yet more anxiety and new challenges to the staff, pupils and governors of the school at a time of great pressure.

The first concern for the school was to help each child take up the role of learner as soon as possible and then to help maintain this role. Nothing we did at George Orwell School was particularly new: we considered our practice in the light of our understanding of troubled children and of good pastoral care and adjusted our practice appropriate.

It is true that many of these children had suffered experiences which appalled us. But in thinking about what the school could do to help them it was important to consider their experience of loss and change. We also considered their previous educational experience and other social factors.

Loss and change

In leaving their homelands the refugee child has often experienced maximum dislocation. Possible losses include:

loss of close and/or extended family members through death or separation

loss of friends through death or separation

loss of home and possessions

loss of homeland, culture and language

Possible traumas experienced:

witnessing violence against parents

witnessing humiliation of parents

witnessing destruction of home

witnessing torture

witnessing violent death

suffering violence against themselves

suffering torture

experiencing parents as powerless to protect

experiencing authority as hostile/ violent

experiencing fear and uncertainty during flight

(From Wagner and Lodge, 1995)

Reflecting on these possible changes and traumas and their implications for the lives of young people was an important first step for reviewing what the school could do to help and as a contribution to staff development in this area.

Previous educational experience

Children had very different experiences of education before arriving in our school. Educational systems differ in different countries: age of starting school; subjects taught, methods of instruction, discipline, ethos of schools, resources, materials and equipment available or used in schools. Some children had experienced fairly harsh regimes and spoke of being pleased to find that teachers did not slap children or use a stick (George Orwell School, 1993). Other important aspects to consider were the ways in which children had been taught. Often they had been in large classes, with few opportunities to take part in practical activities such as art or experiments in science lessons. Many were used to very formal instruction and were unfamiliar with small group work.

In some countries, Somalia for example, schools have been severely disrupted by the war, and many children had not attended formal schools for some time, often years. Other children had experienced severe disruption to their schooling while leaving their country and were only able to receive instruction in refugee camps.

Other factors influencing their lives

For many refugee children, entering a school in Britain can be their first experience of stability for some time. However, other factors may divert and distract them from their studies. For example, many young people learned English faster than other members of the family and were called upon to act as interpreters and spokespeople for their families when dealing with officials. These might include the Home Office and legal advisers to follow up their application for asylum, medical care, housing officials and education officers. This often meant they took time off school. The staff of the school found it hard to resolve the tension between the importance of attendance at school and their sympathy with the families' needs for the services of the children.

It was clear that we needed to understand these extra demands upon the pupils, and from time to time give them support in finding solutions. This meant keeping in touch with the local community groups, and legal services, MPs' advice surgeries and other organisations.

At the time of writing a further serious risk is now affecting many newly-arrived refugee children and their families: the withdrawal of benefits and an entitlement to social housing from the majority of asylum-seekers as a result of the Asylum and Immigration Act 1996. As a result, families may become homeless and hungry, and children lose their rights to school meals, uniform grants and other important benefits (see Chapter Two). The impact on schools' work cannot be predicted with any accuracy, but children are unlikely to find their lives easier as a result of these changes.

This change to benefits entitlement is part of a policy of making the UK unwelcoming to refugees to dissuade them from applying for asylum in this country, in short it is a policy to create a 'fortress Britain' within 'fortress Europe' (Rutter, 1994). In such a climate schools have a greater challenge in trying to create a positive and good induction for individual families and their children in the context of a very unwelcoming public policy.

Developing and maintaining good home-school liaison was important, especially as some children arrived unaccompanied. Some families experienced difficulties with their children after some time in this country. We needed to understand the family's perspectives and hopes for their child alongside the reactions of young persons to their new situation. Sometimes the teachers were able to act as a third party between the young people and their families, especially when the youngsters appeared to be rejecting the family's values and norms. Our role was to help the family understand what was happening, and to find additional sources of help if necessary, usually from within their own community.

It was important to see the support offered by the school as an entitlement. This helped to avoid colleagues concentrating on the horror of what had been done to these children, or seeing them only as victims. The direct support came mainly from the teachers of English as a second language and the form tutors.

We were greatly assisted in our achievements by a generous grant through the Grants for Education Support and Training (GEST) from the Department for Education and Employment (DfEE) for one year, which enabled us to support experimentation, to employ a consultant to help us evaluate our practices and celebrate the achievement of the school as a whole and refugee pupils in particular, through making a video programme, called *Safe in Another Country*, and other special events.

It is useful to describe the processes we found were effective at three levels, while keeping in mind that these levels are interlinked and reinforce one another:

- whole school level
- classroom level and the curriculum
- individual level.

Whole school level

Writing about equal opportunities in our school at about the time when refugees were arriving in large numbers, a Year Nine student said 'I think the school is great the way it is mixed up.' The school was able to build on its experience of good anti-racist educational practice to cope with change. These strengths arose partly because the school was situated in a community which had over many decades welcomed families newly arrived in the country and in the capital and where racial tension had been rare. The school benefited from this and deliberately built upon it. The pupils were explicit in many ways about not accepting racism. We also found from a staff survey that for many of the staff the ethnic diversity of the school population and the strong antiracist ethos was a major reason for wanting to work in the school.

The school already had a positive attitude towards managing changes imposed from outside. It had already taken in its stride becoming part of a newly created local education authority (LEA), taking responsibility for a delegated budget and other powers through Local Management of Schools (LMS). It had adapted its curriculum to ensure that the National Curriculum was introduced as constructively as possible. And it was already familiar with a high pupil turnover.

Staff development and training Training for the staff was an immediate priority. We needed to understand the experience of refugee children: to know about the countries from which they had come, their languages, cultures and educational provision. We needed to know what had been happening in these countries to cause families to leave and to consider the variety of experiences, provenances, journeys and previous education of the children. And we needed to spend time sharing our concerns, thoughts and experiences of working successfully with the children, especially where we had directly addressed their experiences (for example in English, where they wrote autobiographies, and in art, where they painted from their experiences see below).

Staff development resources on refugee education are now more widely available, including video programmes (for example, Safe in Another Country, the video we made in 1993), courses (for example by the Refugee Council), or materials used for training teachers in schools (Wagner and Lodge, 1995), alongside useful books and articles, for example Lodge, 1992; Lodge, 1995; Melzak and Warner, 1992; Rutter, 1994. Many LEAs in London have been running courses to develop the skills and understanding of teachers in schools and of supporting staff in the LEA.

We used expertise from the Refugee Council and Amnesty International, the Minority Rights Group, the Medical Foundation for the Care of Victims of Torture and the National Association for Pastoral Care in Education (NAPCE). We bought in the services of a consultant who had long experience in equal opportunities and EAL work, and we drew on the expertise and growing experience of our own staff.

Induction All children new to a school need a warm welcome and to fit quickly into the school and their own peer group. To provide this welcome schools need to give induction strategies some thought and preparation. Detailed checklists and suggestion can be found in the staff development materials referred to earlier (Wagner and Lodge, 1995). The main features are:

- *The initial interview.* There were practical issues to prepare for, such as using interpreters; knowing the information that will be needed; giving information to the parent or carer; the knowledge and skills required by the interviewer. We used the Head of Year or the Head of EAL. We prepared a video in the seven main languages used in the school, and it gave parents information about the English education system, the school organisation, teaching styles and other useful information.

- *Communication of information to staff.* Teachers of a new pupil required information about the child's first language, country of origin, English language competence, prior educational experience, interests, likes, dislikes and ambitions, special educational needs and important medical information. This was given at the daily morning teachers' briefing session.

- *Induction into class.* Each new child was assigned a 'buddy' on arrival, whose job was to show the new arrival the ropes and to look after her/him for those critical first weeks. Often the buddies had themselves benefited from the befriending system when they came to the school. Wherever possible we used children with the same first language. Their buddy's name was included in the information on the 'Yellow Card' given to all new pupils, along with the new arrival's name, language, country of origin, tutor and form. This card acted as a kind of passport, enabling all staff to get information about the children, when they did not know where they should be, for example, without making them feel more helpless by asking them questions they could not understand or answer. When we reviewed our induction processes, students said that they valued buddies and the use of the yellow card.

- *Reviewing the progress of the refugee child.* At times there could be five new children arriving during one week, and this meant that it was hard to find time to review progress of those who arrived in the preceding weeks as frequently as we would have liked. We aimed to review progress after six weeks and then, if there were no particular concerns, monitoring would take place through the regular termly review of all pupils. In practice, the tutors were alert to any developing difficulties, such as isolation, unhappiness or disorientation and able to take appropriate action. The members of the school were already well known for making people welcome and we now explicitly and frequently celebrated this aspect of our work, in assemblies and in the fortnightly newsletter to parents (which also included a welcome to newcomers by name in every issue). We emphasised the value of diversity of language and culture in the school. Our success may be judged by these comments from pupils in Year Eight and Nine:

As some of the students said:

At this school a good thing is that there are all different people, different religions. You can learn about different people's lives.

I think the thing we do best is we treat everyone the same and teachers take extra care for the people who need it.

If everyone doesn't have the same opportunities everything goes wrong.

I think every class should have different races so that people can help each other.

A persistent difficulty we experienced on admission related to the child's age. Parents unfamiliar with the rigid system of age cohorts were often keen to start children in a lower class. We understood their motives: they wanted their children to have more education because they had missed it, or to allow them more time to learn English. Sometimes we were given false years of birth. There was often little proof of the child's date of birth. For example, one family had three children, all, according to their papers, born on 1st January but in successive years. One child entered the school three times (a long story, not relevant here), presenting evidence of being younger each time. And sometimes we were confused by the family composition: for example, we admitted three children to the same year group, born of two different mothers but the same father and all born within 12 months.

We found it advisable to stick to chronological age groups wherever possible, even if this meant moving children after a few weeks or months. This was partly because the children did find it easier to mix with pupils of their own age in the rigid year system used in Britain. It was also because their entitlements to benefits and education post16 are agerelated and we did not want the children to miss out on any entitlements they might need in the future. Moving a child took place after a great deal of discussion with them and their parents.

Another issue which needed careful handling was that many refugee families did not feel confident about giving information to people employed in public services. We did not ask for a great deal of information about the family, but we did ask about their refugee status, and about the parents and their whereabouts. It was helpful to explain that this information was confidential to the school but needed for monitoring and for supporting the child in school. Our LEA had introduced self-identification of ethnic and religious information some years earlier, and we drew on our experience of this in developing our practice. Asking for information is a question which troubles many teachers, as is evident from the number of times this issue gets raised at training sessions. It would undermine the relationship between schools and families if schools were obliged to pass on such information, as has been hinted recently by the DfEE (DfEE, 1996).

Although many children settled in very quickly there were some who experienced difficulties with school life. A brother and sister from a Polish Romany family told us that they were not allowed to attend school in Poland. They found attendance hard, and more than once the girl was seen during the last lesson of the day playing with a small rubber ball. It took her a while to cope with a full day, and longer to manage a full week. A few refugee children challenged the school in more difficult ways, by behaving in an unacceptable way, often as if they were a great deal younger. There was a tension between being consistent in our behaviour policy and making allowances for these children.

Some of our pupils had come to this country without either of their parents or any other adult carers. The number of unaccompanied children seeking asylum has been rising: from 185 in 1992 to 357 in 1994, and was expected to reach 500 in 1995 (Brown, 1995). Our unaccompanied children were cared for by the local authority, and placed in children's homes or with foster parents. We found it important to spend time making good contacts with the social workers and foster parents (see Chapter Four for more about supporting unaccompanied refugee children).

Once the young person had settled into her/his class, the regular structures of school support, welfare, guidance and reviews were generally sufficient to meet their needs. However, we did need to become acquainted with the particular entitlement of these young people after their compulsory education. We were fortunate to have excellent links with City and Islington College of Further Education, who were very open to hearing about the particular needs of these young people. They were sympathetic to their ambitions and to their need to take a little more time than their peers to achieve educational goals. Young people arriving during the GCSE courses with little or no English language skills were unable to achieve many GCSE passes at 16. It was important for appropriate courses to be provided for them after they left the school.

Many whole school policies already reinforce the work of the school with refugee children. The important ones which were in place or being developed at our school were:

* equal opportunities and antiracism

* home-school liaison

* pastoral care and guidance

* homework policy

* language policy

* antibullying policy

Ensuring that these policies were mutually supportive and interrelated was another important management task.

Classroom level and curriculum

Two aspects of the curriculum are important when considering the experience of refugee children:

> Every night I would go home and pray to God I would learn more English. I couldn't speak to anyone and I couldn't understand. (Chaltu, a 14-year old girl whose family had been killed in Ethiopia.)

> I am at a secondary school in the heart of London. It's an English school where I learn all subjects in English (apart from French). It has been very difficult and hard work for me to learn yet another language, English, after learning French in Kinshasa. It's very hard for me to understand some lessons like science because sometimes there are long words. But I like my lessons because I know they are going to help me in future. My favourite lessons are PE, history and French. (Bolombo Motondo, a 14year old boy from Zaire quoted in Warner, 1995).

This is not the place to examine how to help children acquire English, only to note that for the youngsters who came to our school, like Chaltu and Bolombo, this was the first important learning objective. Although we found ways to help them use their home language, most of the instruction and other learning resources in the school were in English. Examinations are in English. Some of the older pupils forced themselves through GCSE examinations with the aid of a wellthumbed dictionary, motivated by determination to demonstrate what they knew, understood and could do. They achieved particular success in technology and art GCSE in this way, even after a few months.

Helping children develop English competence in a classroom which contained a wide range of competences was a central theme of much of our staff development over several years. Each department was encouraged to develop materials relevant to their subject which newly arrived students could work on immediately. The EAL department developed a 'Yellow Book' of basic information, and supported new arrivals in language classes twice a week, and in some lessons. As there were only three of them and over 150 children, their main task was to help classroom teachers develop skills and strategies to enable students to learn English.

Learning English was essential to learning, but we also encouraged the young people to maintain the use of and contact with their home language. Social and work talk took place in the many of the thirtytwo different first languages of the school. School work was sometime completed in a first language. The librarian took a lot of trouble to find first language reading books for the library. The languages department took a lead in encouraging children to gain qualification in their first or even second language (if it was not English) and in 1994 we were able to introduce Turkish GCSE at Key Stage Four.

Curriculum access through acquiring English language use A child from Bolivia recorded this statement for our video, *Safe in Another Country*: 'All the people know that I am talking two languages and I'm really proud of myself.'

One of the selection criteria for the recruitment of new staff was an understanding of the additional complexity of classrooms that had children at very different stages of English language competence. Partnership teaching between EAL and subject specialists was a particularly productive strategy for staff development, although expensive in staff time. The consultant talked to large numbers of refugee pupils and observed many lessons. She fed back to staff in written form and at training events examples of good practice and information about what the children found to be effective.

Inclusion of refugee related issues in the curriculum In terms of curriculum content, there were two important aspects which we developed in response to the presence of refugee pupils: exploring the existence and condition of refugees in our world and the personal and emotional experience of loss, change and death. Both aspects were felt to be important for all youngsters to explore.

We set out to explore a number of issues relating to the refugees in our world as an important part of the school's curriculum. We looked at human rights, displacement of peoples, how people react to war, to violence and to refugees, the countries of origin of refugee children, and political and media reactions to refugees coming to Britain. All of these themes related to aspects of the National Curriculum, the agreed religious education syllabus and to other parts of the school's curriculum. These themes were developed in the schemes of work for art, religious education, the tutorial programme (Personal and Social Education or PSE), drama, English, history and geography and maths.

Materials exist to help teachers: see for example *We Left Because We Had To* (Rutter, 1996) or *The Dispossessed* (IBT, 1992), Voices (Warner, 1995). We also used *Safe in Another Country*, the video programme we had made at the school.

As part of developing our PSE programme we were already including personal issues about change, loss and death in our curriculum. We developed a unit of work to help young people look at reactions to these experiences, stages of grief and how friends can help. Tutors did not always feel comfortable dealing with such sensitive issues with their class, not all were convinced of the value of such work. However we were able to use experienced staff alongside tutors where support was requested. This work was reinforced by other parts of the curriculum in English, art, religious education and drama.

Autobiography is a particularly valuable tool of empowerment: telling your own story is part of understanding and integrating your reactions into your understanding of your own life. (This point was examined in relation to primary school aged children in Chapter Seven.) It also helps avoid 'accidental' secrecy, that secrecy with which we accidentally collude and which can be prevent children from coming to terms with their experiences. In English lessons autobiography was already part of the work of all Year 11 children. Another useful aspect of the English scheme of work was exploring other people's stories about flight and refugees.

Aziza, a nine year old Somali girl from Barlby Primary School, London W10, showed what her imagination could communicate about her feelings towards her homeland in this poem, which was later featured in the *Times Educational Supplement*:

The Two Azizas

Aziza watches Power Rangers
Every day on the tele.
At night the other Aziza goes
Flying through the sky.

Aziza likes swimming but
She's not very good.
At night the other Aziza
Goes swimming in the ocean
With the big fish.

Aziza never goes on holiday
But the other Aziza
Goes to Somalia every weekend.

Some children found that their work in art drew upon their early experiences of living in different cultures, and in different circumstances. The art teacher encouraged them to bring photographs and artefacts and then they worked with them in a variety of different media: video, photography, interactive programmes on a CD ROM, as well as paint and collage. Some of the resulting art work by refugee children was profoundly disturbing to see: images of weapons, death, fear and of violent disturbances were frequent. But many of them had found a 'voice' to explore and retell their experiences.

Dursa, a 16 year old boy from Ethiopia, described how his father had been shot, his mother stayed to bury him and he had to walk, to avoid the land mines, to Sudan which took 27 days.

> These things that I told you are still very, very fresh in my mind. I do remember them. Art is a very interesting subject to me. I a small piece of paper you can describe all sorts of things, lots of things about war, you know, prison, anything about what happens in the world at the moment or in the past.

Caring for the Individual

One plane, one journey took me away from my life. (Bosnian girl, 14 years.)

138

At the level of the individual child the staff found that they needed to develop strategies and understanding in two aspects of their work: the general guidance and welfare of each individual pupil, and extra support for those children who were very troubled by their experiences.

General care for individual. Starting at a new school can be a difficult experience for any young person, and the support which the tutor and other staff could give was crucial for the youngsters. Our main allies were the other pupils: the 'buddy' and the other children who befriended the newcomer.

The role of the tutor, supported by the Head of Year and the EAL teachers, was critical. The depth of knowledge gained by the most effective tutors about their students, their experiences, and by their strategies for helping them was impressive. They were often the point of contact for parents, contacting them at times of absence of the pupils, persisting through difficulties of communication, explaining the peculiarities of the English education system, listening to the parents' hopes and fears for their children. Tutors acted as champions of their students, defending them against injustices, explaining their learning difficulties to their teachers, checking that homework was understood, and supporting them in completing it. The role of the tutor was being developed over a number of years, and remained a priority during this time.

This kind of support was often a novel feature of school for refugee students, many of whom had experienced large classes, formal systems with strict, even brutal discipline to enforce obedience. As Ali, a 14year old boy from Somalia, explained on the video *Safe in Another Country*:

> I'm used to going to a school where there'd be a stick over you and actually coming to a school in London where a teacher is not carrying a stick and is not a hundred per cent strict was ... [pause] ... it was good thing to find.

And Cecelia, a 16 year old girl from Bolivia who had been in the school less than three years, described her experience of the teachers:

They help you a lot, a thing that in my country I think that they didn't do. When a person didn't understand anything, didn't speak English, they are trying to give you all their attention. So that is good. That is what I like about this school.

Teachers found their own foreign language skills called upon. At different times in the determined efforts to communicate and make connection with pupils who did not speak English, French (especially for children from Zaire), German (trying to work with Polish Roma family), Spanish (with the youngsters from South American), Turkish, and Italian (for some Somali and Ethiopian children who had passed through Italy) were all brought into play. Our own efforts at foreign languages were often very puny in contrast to the achievements of the youngsters themselves.

Refugee students needed particular guidance for careers, further education and their employment future. The Islington Careers Service took a lead in investigating and promoting information about entitlements of refugees and published a useful handbook. Our careers adviser worked closely with the school's Careers Co-ordinator and Head of EAL, as well as with the local further education college (as mentioned above) to ensure that the pupils received the proper guidance and support in their post16 decisions and choices.

Special support for troubled children While most children adjust to their new school and come to terms with their previous, sometimes horrific, experiences, a number remain troubled and are unable to develop as learners, and they may need the help of specialists. The security and routines of school are therapeutic experiences in themselves which should not be underestimated. The interest of concerned and supportive adults is also important, especially where parents may not be able to give adequate support (because they are absent, or have their own difficulties with coping).

Teachers, who spend their lives involved with children, can often find themselves so horrified by the experiences of refugee children that they cannot see beyond their own reaction of shock. It can be tempting to overuse the description of such children as 'traumatised'. An important part of staff development is to understand what will help a young person. The following describes some factors which help or hinder a refugee child in making the change.

Factors which can help a child to cope with the transition
- parent/s present and able to care emotionally and materially

- parent/s understanding, affirming and supportive of the child/ young person

- other adults understanding, affirming and supportive of the child/ young person

- child understands reasons for exile

- child has good links with homeland and with any remaining relations

- child is in good health

- child has previous educational experience

Factors which make things more difficult:
- the inverse of all of the above

- trauma such as:

     child has witnessed extremes of violence

     child's experience of leaving was stressful and difficult

     child was and/or is separated from parents

(From Wagner and Lodge, 1995.)

It was important to be alert for signs which might indicate difficulties in making the transition into a new life, usually these were changes in behaviour, or responses to triggers or obsessive repetitions. A particularly useful booklet is *Wise before the Event* (Yule and Gold, 1993). This was sent to every school on publication, and describes symptoms of post traumatic stress disorder (PTSD).

- the event is persistently reexperienced in thoughts, dreams of flashbacks; the child engages in persistent repetitive play

- persistent avoidance of stimuli associated with the trauma or numbing of general responsiveness; extreme distress is triggered by a specific stimulus

- signs of increased psychological arousal such as disturbed sleep and poor concentration

- 'It is now recognised that PTSD is a normal reaction to an abnormal situation. Children need to be reassured about this and that they can be helped'. (Yule and Gold, 1993).

One boy became obsessive about washing, not being touched, and making sure that he had his back to the wall at all times. He appeared to experience no sense of risk or danger, riding his bicycle to Piccadilly Circus after midnight on one occasion, leaving it unchained in the care of a total stranger, and exploring this environment until the police picked him up. He was surprised not to be able to recover his bike. His father resisted our attempts to secure specialist help, despite involvement of the educational psychologist and mental health experts. It took time, but eventually he was placed for assessment.

A headteacher of a nearby primary school which had a number of refugee children on roll, rang me in alarm one day. Some of his refugee children had appeared to run amok one afternoon, and had been quite unable to settle, and the whole school had been disrupted by their wild behaviour. The trigger for this behaviour was the local police helicopter circling overhead.

Many behaviours by refugee children needed to be kept under review, but were not generally severe enough to require special measures such as referral for specialist help. These included playing with children of a much younger age and drawing or painting very violent, or very serene scenes, in art. It was important to differentiate our reactions to the child's experiences from their reactions.

It was important to be aware of what services were available to support the school or the individual child who needed more than time and the support and care which the school offered in a general way: these included education welfare officers, educational psychologists, local health and psychiatric services, and specialist agencies such as the Medical Foundation for the Care of Victims of Torture.

Public perceptions

As the school worked explicitly and overtly to ensure that the young refugees were able to take a full part in school life, and as we published what we had learned, and gave talks and led seminars, were the subject of radio broadcasts and newspaper articles, the school gained some celebrity for its work. This had some curious, and not always welcome, outcomes. Following a particularly interesting programme in December 1994 on Radio Four called Lost Childhoods, a number of members of the public contacted the school to offer a home for a refugee child for Christmas (prompting one to think 'a refugee comes to this country not just for Christmas, but for life'), a cheque for £10 and a cottage piano for which the transport costs were also paid.

We had to protect and screen requests from the media for interviews and articles about refugees. Many children and their families were very nervous about attracting any publicity which might rebound on members of their family still in their homeland, and would only agree to take part if their real names were not used. But journalists in pursuit of an interesting angle sometimes over stepped bounds of decency: a video producer wanted to shadow a recently arrived refugee, including in his home, to record his reactions because he thought it would make an interesting programme. Another child was requested by a television producer to symbolise all refugees at the 50th anniversary of the liberation of the Netherlands. Both requests were refused, and we developed a shorthand way of referring to such requests as *rentarefugee*. We felt able to support media projects which would highlight the situation of the young people, not portray them, or the school, as helpless pawns at the mercy of a cruel destiny, and where the journalist or interviewer understood where there might be areas of sensitivity.

The presence of a large number of refugee children in the school confronted the school with the new conflicts, realities and values of the market place in education. This new context was created by the introduction in the Education Reform Act 1988 with its emphasis on parental choice, LMS and schools' resourcing based largely on pupil numbers. The school had already taken a decision not to go for superficial marketing changes such as introducing uniform, or to present the school as other than it was with its lively and challenging multicultural environment.

Three features of the new education market reinforced each other, creating a difficulty for recruitment from which it is hard to see a principled way out.

First, schools with small rolls are vulnerable to disabling limits on resources and destabilising forces as the funding follows the fluctuations of pupil numbers. The competitive market context encourages schools to make themselves appear more attractive to parents, possibly by defining its own specialism or 'market niche'. Our speciality was working with refugees.

> Yet an emphasis on provision for Black and bilingual students carries with it a risk of alienating many of those middleclass families who are valued in the market place by schools generally... (Gewirtz, Ball, and Bowe, 1995, p 152.)

> A further aspect of choicemaking which tends to be neglected in the literature on parental choice but which emerges from our own data is that parents seem to make choices on the basis of perceived class and in some instances racial composition of schools. (Ibid. p 184.)

Second, parents are encouraged to view raw performance data as comparative information on which to judge schools. The true achievements of the young people and their schools remains hidden while no indication is given of the pupils' starting points, or their expected progress. This is what is known as 'the value-added'. League tables implicitly place a high value on those achieving five A-C grades at GCSE. Our own and the LEA analyses showed that comparing known ability on intake, our students achieved comparable GCSE performances. Despite our own best efforts at publicising the achievements of all our students this picture was a complex one, and was not even well understood by members of the education committee.

Third, research suggests that in the new competitive context schools value pupils differently based on how likely they are to enhance a school's league table performance with minimal investment (especially of teacher time, but also other resources, such as specialist materials). Refugees require high investment of these kinds, and their performance will usually depress the school's league table performance, because they present raw scores. The most robust schools, those with secure resourcing can avoid taking refugees, not least by being full of pupils who have made choices with their parents at eleven. The more vulnerable schools, who simply need more children on roll to enhance their resourcing situation have less control. The segregatory effects of the market contain a racial dimension. Ethnic minority children, including refugees, are disproportionately represented among the most economically disadvantaged sections of the population and so they are more likely also to be disproportionately represented in undersubscribed schools (Gewirtz et al., 1995).

The circularity of this trap is evident: the school has spaces, and so refugees enrol. As a result the school remains unpopular because it does not appeal to those who are best at exercising such choice as the market provides them with, and the school cannot demonstrate its achievements in an attractive way. The school therefore continues to have spare capacity. The economic consequences of this cycle are a serious management problem, and George Orwell suffered acutely from them.

Many children had had to leave their home country because of political activities in which their parents and other family members were involved. Feelings ran high, especially where people had experienced the death of members of their family as a result of these struggles. It was important to keep a feel for relationships between Turkish children and those who described themselves as Kurdish. We were fortunate to have a Turkish member of staff, who, on one occasion when feelings and accusations ran high, worked sensitively with all groups, providing them with a forum for the expression of their views, and with a sense that school was a place to debate their differences, but not to allow their differences to get in the way of their learning.

On another occasion, I offended a group of Turkish youngsters by referring to Kurdistan in the school's newsletter. They came to see me, armed with a map, to prove that there was no such place. The debate was lively, but friendly. I apologised for any offence, but pointed out that it existed in the minds of many Kurdish people, and that their aspirations could not be ignored.

I was quite unable to resolve a difference between two groups of Muslims at the annual Eid party: one group, mainly Bengali, and fundamentalist, strongly disapproved of music being played at this party. The others, mostly Turkish, argued that without music it would really not be a party. I suggested a good liberal compromise: 20 minutes with music, 20 minutes without, but the argument was only laid to rest when afternoon school recommenced.

Conclusions

Schools working with refugees are often isolated, because the children are spread unevenly among schools. And where there is only a small number of refugee children in one school, there is a danger of their being isolated and seen as a problem. In London, many LEAs have started to set up networks to support schools and teachers working with refugees. In some local authorities the vision has gone further, and links have been made with housing, social services and equal opportunities departments.

Whether this kind of support exists or not, schools can play a significant part in helping refugee children become effective learners within our education system. Some young refugees in Sweden suggested six valuable and supportive aspects of schools (Melzak, 1992).

What refugee children say they value and find supportive about school
• teachers who made some adjustment in their teaching methods

• teachers who asked them about themselves

• teachers who made an effort to include refugee children's experiences into the curriculum

• teachers who took racism seriously

• schools which invited members of the refugee community into the school

• teachers who came to special cultural occasions in the refugee community.

The spirit and courage of refugee children and their families, in this country and abroad, has deepened my understanding of the world, what people do to each other, and of the importance of taking account of children's experiences and emotions, of hearing their voice, to help them in school. These sentiments are reflected by Senait from Eritrea.

I was born in Hashase in Eritrea. When I was very young my family left Eritrea because there was a big war going on so it was not safe to live in my country. We had to get away. I lived in a village in Libya. My house was not very small and it was a good place to live because all the people in the village were friendly to each other and they helped each other. People shared their problems with each other and that's how they solved their problems...

On the flight to London I thought about what it was going to be like in England. Was it going to be the same as Libya? Were the people friendly? What would happen when we arrived at Heathrow airport?

I don't know what is going to happen in the future but one day I would like to get married and have a family. I would like to see my children have a good education and respectable jobs. I would teach them to live together peacefully and to give help to those who need it. (Wagner and Lodge, 1995, p 47)

CHAPTER NINE

Refugee Students' Experiences of the UK Education System

Jeremy McDonald

Young refugees and asylum seekers aged between 14 and 19 years old have been identified as a group who have very particular educational needs and who frequently have difficulties gaining appropriate education. Teachers in schools and colleges, and providers of educational guidance and other services for refugees have recognised that the needs and circumstances of this group are insufficiently understood and that it is necessary to develop services which are capable of identifying and meeting their needs. Accordingly, their experiences into the UK education system[1] were examined, and refugee students in the 14-19 year-old age group attending schools and colleges in London chosen as the subject of the research.

The vulnerable situation of many young refugees is due to a number of interlinked factors. Their arrival and the difficult circumstances of resettlement in this country occur during and in the aftermath of experiences of disruption, dislocation, loss, and often of trauma, associated with flight from persecution and danger. As they try to resume their interrupted education they are faced with the challenges of adjusting to a new and unfamiliar education system, of adapting to different cultural norms and expectations, and of learning a new language of survival and of instruction. These processes of adaptation, learning and adjustment take place in the midst of the uncertainties and practical difficulties of resettlement.

For refugee teenagers the transition has to be made during their adolescence. The 'normal' difficulties of adjusting to new adult roles and responsibilities are compounded and complicated by the shock of adjusting to a new culture and environment in the context of unfamiliar peer pressures – pressures which are often competitive, and sometimes aggressive or even violent. Furthermore, the transition occurs during a decisive period in their educational careers, as they arrive in this country just before, just after, or just as they are completing their secondary schooling in educational systems which are different from the British system.

Some new arrivals may have missed significant parts of their education due to war, civil strife, persecution, dislocation and flight. Some may have received no primary or secondary education at all, or very little; others will have missed months or years of education during protracted periods of flight and insecurity; and some will have spent periods of time attending schools or classes in refugee camps or schools in other countries before arriving in Britain.

Relative compatibility between other education systems and the British system will affect the transition in different ways. Some refugees will have learned English or used it as a language of education; others will not. Some may be highly literate in more than one language, whereas others may have limited or even no literacy in their first language. Examination and qualifications systems may be relatively similar or extremely different, and transferring students' attainments may or may not accord with the levels of the age-related progression system in use in British schools. For some of those at the older end of the 14-19 age range, the transition may occur fortuitously as they have completed their secondary education in their home countries. Others are faced with the difficulty of trying to find a place in a school or a course in a college which can help them to compensate for the education which they have missed.

As a group, young refugees are heterogeneous both in terms of educational experience and achievement, and also in terms of background – coming from a range of social classes, ethnic, national and religious groups, and from both rural and urban backgrounds. The extent of family, community and other support to which they have recourse in this country is also very varied, ranging from the extreme isolation and vulnerability of unaccompanied children and 'young carers' taking parental responsibility for small family/sibling groups, to those living with parents or in families who have direct links with relatively established refugee community groups in the UK.

Despite their heterogeneity, the vulnerability of their circumstances and the crucial educational stage at which they arrive, young refugees share a set of common and urgent needs: for effective and accessible educational advice and guidance, for initial/diagnostic assessment as a basis for establishing continuity between previous education and current/future learning programmes, and for specific kinds of support to assist them in being able to resume, reconstruct, or even, in some cases, to begin their educational careers on their arrival in the UK.

Young refugees need to be able to make informed choices about education in a system which is highly differentiated and which has been undergoing far-reaching structural changes during the last decade and more. For those who enrol in schools, the imminence of GCSE exams poses immediate and difficult questions about their effective participation in Key Stage Four of the National Curriculum and in GCSE classes and exams. For those who enrol in colleges, there is a wide and confusing array of courses and qualifications to choose between, many of them with only very recently introduced new forms of accreditation and assessment.

They need to be able to learn English rapidly as a language of survival, of social interaction and of education. Unfortunately, as the research shows, there is great variability in both schools and colleges in the quality and extent of English language provision for speakers of additional languages (EAL), with the result that one of the most obvious and immediate needs of many refugees – the acquisition of English for survival and for effective participation in education – is often not met.

They also share with all students the need for a variety of forms of learning support – whose availability is extremely variable. Some students interviewed during the course of the research progressed well within the system without additional support or specialised guidance of any kind. Some received support when they needed it or at crucial moments, allowing them to adapt, progress and achieve. Others who received no additional support endured frustration, repetition, isolation and sometimes hostility, and yet still progressed and achieved – eventually. Those without support were often struggling against numerous obstacles, not least the seeming indifference to their needs of the education system. Others again were trying to get into provision more suited to their needs, and some seemed unlikely to stay in education at all.[2]

The context of legislative change

The research was carried out during a period of enormous change in the education system. The introduction of the National Curriculum and other changes brought about by the Education Reform Act 1988 and the Education Act 1992 have significantly altered the ways in which schools are organised, funded and controlled. Schools have been encouraged to opt out of local authority control and to acquire new financial and administrative autonomy. In the post-school sector, the Further and Higher Education Act 1992 removed Further Education (FE) and sixth form colleges from local authority control. Since April 1993 the FE sector has been transformed by the 'incorporation' of colleges as autonomous corporate bodies funded by the Further Education Funding Council, and by the merging of many adult and community education centres into the new college corporations.

The introduction of the National Curriculum with its four Key Stages in schools, and the recent establishment of the tripartite curriculum framework of the GCSE/A Level, GNVQ, and NVQ routes of progression in the post-school phase (with a vocational route also being established from age 14 in schools), have created a potentially more coherent but still very complicated and confusing system of qualifications and educational progression in this country.

The traditional divisions between academic and vocational education and training have not been bridged by the reforms or by the introduction of GNVQs (General National Vocational Qualifications), and the vexed question of parity of esteem between the vocational and academic routes and their associated qualifications remains unresolved. A Levels, in the elite academic track, continue to dominate and thus to distort a system for which the claim is made that it consists of several but equal tracks (Feingold et al, 1990; Wolf, 1994).

A significant effect of the reforms has been that the 14-19 phase of education is increasingly being seen as a continuum. The National Curriculum Key Stages are aligned with post-16 academic and vocational tracks in the newly evolved national qualifications system. The national targets for Education and Training (NETTS) are designed to promote increased staying-on and participation rates in post-16 education. The issues of 14-19 progression and the 16-plus qualifications system are the subject of the recent review by Sir Ron Dearing (March 1996), of a first report by the House of Commons Education Committee on Education and Training of 14-19 year olds (February 1996), and of Labour Party policy documents which are shadowing these developments.

This new emphasis upon the 14-19 phase of education has focused attention upon such issues as the need for adequate systems of advice, guidance and initial assessment, for the creation of routes of progression between phases of education and across the tracks of the qualifications system, and for learning support systems which can complement and compensate for more flexible modes of curriculum delivery. If they are well resourced, these developments have the potential to improve opportunities for all students, including refugee students and bilingual students. They could provide their needs and their educational choices could be enhanced.

While the attention being focused upon 14-19 education may stimulate further progress towards greater flexibility and transferability, the academic/vocational divide and the notorious lack of compatibility between different UK qualifications and awards remain as persistent barriers to the flexibility and choice which it was claimed the reforms would deliver. The new qualifications framework has the potential to offer students choices of transfer between the tracks and of combining elements, units or modules from different qualifications in different tracks. However, this kind of flexibility is only partially developed. The flexible and much more extensive systems of learning support which are necessary to underpin the new system are not developed either, nor are they adequately funded.

Social Security changes, introduced as a clause in the Asylum and Immigration Act 1996, have also impeded students in further education from completing courses.

An education marketplace – choice versus selection

As well as these tendencies towards continuity and collaboration across the secondary and tertiary phases of education, there are others. The experiences of refugee students should also be seen in the context of increasing competition for higher achieving students between education providers (between schools, between school sixth forms and colleges, and between colleges), and the restrictive effects that competition and the creeping return of selection have upon educational choice .

Market conditions, it is claimed, will enhance choice and diversity in education, and the government's recently published *Charters for Education* (1993, 1994) aim to guarantee the rights of the citizen/ consumer to informed choice in relation to educational opportunities. The charters emphasise the raising of standards, monitoring progress, and widening diversity and choice in education through the provision of reliable and accessible information to parents and students. Both schools and colleges are required to provide the kind of information about their provision and curriculum that would make citizens' choices meaningful.

However, the confidence and know-how to be able to benefit from the availability of choice are unlikely to be among the competencies of newly arrived refugee families, and without proper access to well informed and up-to-date advice and guidance, they will remain excluded from the rights supposedly associated with entitlement to choice.

Evidence is accumulating that rather than offering what the charters seek to invoke, market conditions and tensions are contributing to the increasing fragmentation of provision, exacerbating greater social segregation in education – 'Schools may become *more* rather than less polarised in terms of their reputation and social class (and ethnic) intake.' (Smith and Noble, 1995).

As well as accentuating inequalities, competition between providers sets up an immediate tension between choice on the part of the potential user of educational services seeking to exercise rights, entitlement and choice in order to find the most appropriate provision for her/ his needs, and selection on the part of the provider seeking to recruit 'quick learners', 'easy successes' – students who will attain qualifications rapidly and with minimal additional support.

Under current market conditions, students requiring additional resources to achieve their potential, may be considered by schools and colleges as being more expensive learners. Despite the evident academic success of many refugee students, they may be liable to depress an institution's position in published league tables of academic achievement. For these reasons refugee students may be excluded by processes of selection.

The pupils and students who live in vulnerable circumstances and in insecure and temporary housing may also be thought likely to bring down other indicators of institutional success such as attendance. As a result, many refugee students are enrolled in 'underachieving schools', an issue discussed in more detail in Chapter One. Current Social Security legislation restricting access of asylum seekers to benefits, housing and other services will increase the vulnerability and enforced mobility of refugees. This is likely further to exclude young refugees from adequate and continuous education, since insecure and temporary housing will cause them to have to move locality and find alternative schools with increasing frequency.

The effects of the multifarious changes brought about by recent legislation and by increasing social inequalities are still being absorbed in different ways in different parts of the secondary and further education sectors. The negative effects of the changes, together with increasingly restrictive immigration legislation and the tightening of restrictions on asylum seekers at national and European levels, have contributed to the creation of a policy framework which tends to diminish rather than to recognise and protect the rights of refugees.

Effects of recent changes on provision for refugees

A direct consequence of recent legislation has been the reduction in the influence of local authorities, and especially their role in providing co-ordinated forms of support for students and professional advice and in-service training for teachers. This has affected provision and the range of support available for pupils and students with additional needs, including refugee students. The policies and initiatives of local education authorities which had been developed in order to assist schools and colleges to respond effectively to the language and learning needs of bilingual students have been curtailed as a result of recent legislation and reductions in Section 11 (Home Office) funding.

The current scarcity of properly trained staff to provide language support is commented on in a recent HMI report on Section 11 provision: 'The pool of teachers and assistants trained for Section 11 work some ten or twenty years ago, when well-designed training courses were more numerous, is now reducing in size although the demand for the kinds of support provided by such teachers continues to be strong' (HMI, 1993).

The scaling down of Section 11 funding and the short time-scale of projects which do receive funding, are currently reducing the capacity of schools, colleges, LEAs and other providers to meet the needs of bilingual students at a time when the demand for EAL courses and support is increasing. Alternative forms of funding at the moment appear to be neither available nor accessible enough for educational purposes for providers to be able to plug the emerging gaps in existing provision, much less to extend the provision required to meet growing needs.

Provision in the FE sector has also been reduced by the merging of many adult and community education centres into the newly incorporated colleges. The current very serious shortage of EAL provision in London, is illustrated by the comment of an FE college Education Guidance Co-ordinator interviewed in the survey:

> Every day there are at least five people who come in here wanting English courses. All we can do is put them on waiting lists until they can apply for a course next September. They just drift from college to college....

These local trends reflect a wider consequence of legislative changes in education – a fragmentation and diminishment of such consensus as had previously existed on the range of policies and practices needed for supporting students from minority ethnic groups in education. (Rutter, 1994)

Resources for supporting students in education so that both their entitlements and potential might be more fully realised in the form of marketable qualifications and achievements have diminished. Local services have also been fragmented and reduced which has made co-ordination of support services more difficult. For refugee students this means barriers inhibiting their prospects for educational continuity and success, and fewer educational opportunities which would allow them to become self-sufficient earners and producers in their adoptive society.

Patterns of participation and progression of refugee students

The pattern of progression and achievement of refugee students, according to the experience of those who were interviewed, reflect some of the trends of participation, progression and achievement of minority ethnic groups identified in recent research on ethnic minorities in Britain (Jones 1993). The period of time taken to qualify is longer than for other students due to a number of factors, including language difficulties, lack of EAL provision, lack of language and learning support and a lack of appropriate provision generally. Refugee students may, like other bilingual and minority ethnic students, be channelled into lower level sets, courses and/or qualifications (CRE, 1992).

In addition, young refugees face other barriers due to the fact that previous educational achievements and qualifications taken abroad are seldom recognised in this country, they may have to repeat educational stages, requalify in the UK system, or restart at a lower stage on the progression ladder.

Patterns of disrupted education before and after arrival

All those interviewed in the research had suffered disruption to their education by moving between countries and changing education systems in mid-career. The education of several had been significantly dislocated before they left their home countries because of war or civil strife.

> First I was at a village school; then we had to move because of the trouble, so I missed a year. When I was 11, I got a scholarship to a secondary school in another town. I was there for three years but I

left in the middle of the third year because we had to move again because of the trouble. So I missed three years of my secondary schooling.

In Somalia I didn't go to school for four and a half years. I went to primary school when I was 7 for four months and then we had to leave because of the war. We tried to get to Ethiopia but we couldn't get in. For two years we lived under the trees in a place between Ethiopia and Somalia.

Seven respondents had temporarily continued their education for brief periods in countries where they had stayed during a protracted process of flight before their arrival in the UK. One had been to 12 schools in Sri Lanka.

We had to move all the time. The army occupied, and we moved away, away, away ...... and finally I got here.

He attended school for one year in Germany while living with his uncle, and then was eventually able to join his father in London where, before going to college, he spent two years in secondary school.

It was pretty terrible, but it was better than Germany. I wouldn't blame anyone – I just couldn't fit. It took two years to improve my English. There was no extra help.

He had learned some English in Sri Lanka and considered that this grounding allowed him to make reasonably good progress in the UK education system – '*I think I've done well considering the situation.*' At the time of the interview he was in the second year of a Science and Maths A Level course in an FE Sixth Form Centre, and was expecting to do well enough to take up the offer of a place at Imperial College, London, to study Engineering.

Access to education in UK – delay, discontinuity, low expectations

For many refugee students such patterns of disruption and discontinuity are also a major feature of their educational experience after their arrival in the UK. Lack of advice and guidance, difficulty in finding school and college places, lack of appropriate FE courses, inadequate or non-existent initial assessment, lack of learning and language support, the restrictive effects of social security regulations, and low expectations on the part of admissions tutors and teaching staff, all added to the educational discontinuities and disruption already experienced by recently arrived refugees.

Lack of access to advice and guidance about educational opportunities means that refugee students' choices are often arbitrary and ill-informed, with the result that in many cases access to appropriate provision and subsequent progress is blocked and delayed.

> We did not receive any information about the education in the UK when we arrived and that's why I kept going from one course to another for the first three months.

> At first my sister liked the school. But there is not enough support for English. If you don't speak English they leave you alone. It is not good for her because she has no friends there. It is difficult to find an alternative place.

> It is hard to get a place in college. It is easier in school. I applied in October to a college for a business course, but I didn't get a reply for four or five months. I started a language course but it was not the right level for me. Then I applied to a different college for a proper education but I still could not find any.

Students in the sample had difficulties in finding appropriate places in both schools and colleges. Anecdotal evidence of significant numbers of refugee students being refused school places is reflected in the research through the experience of twin sisters from Sudan who applied to a local school to do GCSEs. They were interviewed, but a week later were told that the school was full. 'If they didn't have any places, why did they give us an interview?' They would have liked to have known. They suspected that they were not accepted because the school was unwilling or unable to provide for their language learning needs. Having arrived in the UK in February, and following this initial refusal in March, it was not until the end of the summer term that they found places for one month in another school, before going to a further school the following September – a frustrating period of nearly seven months – during which time: 'We just stayed at home.'

Those applying for further education found that college admission and initial assessment systems often appeared to be arbitrary and subject to bureaucratic delay. Some students had to go through lengthy processes of applying to several different institutions before being accepted.

In post-compulsory education, financial difficulties, poverty, lack of availability of study awards and problems encountered in trying to study part-time while claiming benefits also contributed to difficulties of access and progression. For those who reach 19 before they have acquired marketable qualifications, social security regulations create immediate barriers against becoming self-sufficient

> I have had a problem with my benefit since I was 19 in March. When I was at school everything was fine, it wasn't that bad, but going to college is difficult. I am studying part time at college, but the DSS say it should be less hours. But even if I do less hours they say I am not entitled for any further or higher education and that I have to apply for a grant. They say I have to be an unemployed person.
>
> I don't want to stop my education. I don't have enough qualifications or experience. I can't work unless it's cleaning or something like that. I want to do further education because I'm still young. I feel worried at the moment. My sisters are doing fine at school, but maybe they might have some problems, because one of them will be 19 next year.

The research also revealed that many refugee students coming from many different countries resumed their education at a lower level than that at which it had been broken off in their home countries. (This kind of discontinuity was noted, particularly in relation to mathematics.) Inadequate initial assessment, different codes of behaviour, and the age-related progression system in British schools combined in different ways to accentuate discontinuities for students transferring into the system. Three examples show this:

> I would have been in the Upper School now if I had been born four days earlier. The maths is too easy and the other subjects are more basic than what I did in Algeria.

I found it very easy. I couldn't believe that 14-year-olds were doing this low level work. People were not pushing you to your extreme – 'Just do the work and that's enough.

'At first I thought the freedom was great, but a few years ago when I started to study seriously, I realised something had happened. We had lowered ourselves down. 'What kind of grade would I have got in Kenya?' I thought.'

Evidence from this research indicates that, contrary to the expectation in some quarters that refugee students may negatively affect academic league tables, many are very successful eventually, and in many cases despite lack of advice and support. Among the many obstacles that they have to overcome are the negative attitudes of some teaching staff, attitudes which include ignorance from lack of awareness, and which range through low expectations to 'deficit model' assumptions about the learning capacities of bilingual students. As one student put it:

We study double. We have to work four times as hard as the British students, but no one recognises this. It is not acknowledged. I had to work so hard to get a B in an essay. The teachers knew the end result of my work but they didn't know what went into it. At the end of the day a D is what I got in my A Levels. With that much effort, if I'd had some support, that D could have been converted into a B or C.

Because I was a foreigner, with a different accent, and a different way of presenting things, the sixth form teachers were always saying I shouldn't be unrealistic in my expectations, that I should think of alternatives like non-academic training courses. I was only given the PCAS form (for applying to a polytechnic) not the UCCA form for applying for university.

If I'd had more support at A Level I could have done better at the polytechnic or gone to another university. This would have given me better chances in the job market. For example, now I can't go on to do Clinical Psychology. It adds to the disadvantage of being a foreigner, a refugee – as it is we have so many disadvantages.

Low expectations on the part of school and college staff, and uninformed attitudes which tended to equate language learning needs with a lack of academic potential, also conspired to place refugee students on inappropriate courses or in exam groups where they were condemned to waste valuable time and resources in unprofitable repetition.

> I actually argued with them. I was saying that I didn't have any maths difficulties – I'm capable of doing well. Finally they thought the highest grade I would get was a C. But I got a D instead, after spending time with a group who were only supposed to get E instead of higher grades.

In schools with setting systems, some EAL staff were combating the kinds of practices which tended to allocate bilingual students to bottom sets where they were placed among students with learning and behavioural problems – 'It is a battle to get some of our bilingual students into top sets in Maths and Science.'

Similar practices were evident in further education where, because their English language level did not allow them access to the full range of mainstream courses, some students were channelled into lower level general vocational courses which were irrelevant to their previous attainments and current aspirations.

Support for students' learning

A 'young carer' commented on the kind of choice, based on her own hard-won experience, that she would make on behalf of younger siblings in her care: 'In choice of school you have to weigh up the educational standards of the school and the level of support that is provided. I would go for support.'

She also emphasised the importance of flexible support responsive to individual need.

> All students, all refugee students, are different. They don't all need language support, but all need some kind of support. They need tailored support suited to their individual needs. This means consulting the students and thinking about progression. Diagnosis

and assessment don't necessarily happen – if you don't have a problem they consider you're OK.

Unfortunately, as the research showed, this kind of flexible and responsive support was the exception. Awareness of the circumstances and the frequently traumatic nature of the experiences that young refugees had undergone had informed the design of induction and support systems in some institutions only.

Where schools had developed induction systems for newly arrived refugee and other bilingual students, both students and staff agreed that an induction process combining diagnostic assessment, language support and tutorial guidance was the most effective way of supporting the integration of these students into the mainstream curriculum in a phased and flexible way. One student commented:

> There was definitely enough support in the school. You could approach teachers with any problems. They teach everything in induction and then move you to classes when you are ready. The mainstream class was fine. The support teachers came into the class to help if we asked them to come. We went to the induction room for homework help if we needed it.

One school, Hampstead School in North West London, has developed a system of support and induction, and a homework club, as part of a co-ordinated initiative for refugee pupils in the school known as 'Children of the Storm'.[3] Staff and sixth form volunteers collaborate in welcoming and providing support for refugee students, and refugee issues form an important part of the curriculum for all students in the school. An 18 year-old Albanian refugee acknowledged the good fortune which brought him to the school.

> First we were like completely strangers but after a week we were part of the school. It was something strange to come to this school... because before nobody came to the sixth form who couldn't speak English. Everybody helped. It was to them very interesting, it was strange – so they all rushed to help. Everybody was saying – 'Do you understand? Do you want any help?' The teachers, too, were very nice – 'Do you understand? Do you understand?

I know I was lucky. What I liked most was being friendly, trying to help. It was a big support because you feel stranger, like a total stranger in this place – and when you feel confident like nobody hates you and nobody is taking you as some kind of alien, so you just get free and speak yourself.

Other models of support, such as the Horn of Africa After-school Support Group at South Camden Community School in London, seek to promote the educational welfare and integration of particular groups of refugee pupils and students in a school and its immediate locality. The group meets twice a week in the school library (a light and spacious area which is conducive to study), and provides a regular occasion when students, mostly from the school but also from neighbouring schools and colleges, can get help and support from adults – tutors and volunteers who include staff from the Camden Language and Support Service Refugee Team and refugee community representatives offering students' first languages. The support group addresses a wide range of needs – academic, linguistic, social, cultural, personal, emotional and practical.

The group consists largely of students from the Horn of Africa, and therefore it acknowledges and encourages a sense of cultural identity. Other refugee groups (such as Afghan pupils) are also represented and members are encouraged to and do bring friends and classmates to the group. As many of the young refugees attending the support group are unaccompanied children and young carers looking after younger siblings, there is co-ordination with the Camden Family Service Unit and other agencies to provide them with support.

In stark contrast to these responsive systems, other schools attended by refugee students in the research sample simply left new arrivals to survive as best they could, either with no support, or perhaps with a token hour or two in an EAL withdrawal group. This meant that some newly arrived refugee pupils had to fend for themselves as these comments indicate:

There was no guidance, no induction. I was treated exactly like an English student on my first day at school and after that as well.

They just put me in a class that had space in it.

I stayed quiet. I did nothing for one month. If they ask any question, I don't know, it's too hard. If I want anything, I can't ask, can't talk to them...

Insufficiency in the quality and level of language and learning support provided was a key feature of the experience of many of the students in the sample. Some 47 per cent found the level of support they received to be unsatisfactory, and the experience of support of a further 24 per cent of students was 'mixed'.

Students also commented on the positive and negative features of different models of language support, including separate provision, withdrawal groups, in-class support, drop-in workshops, peer support, first language support, and after-school provision.

They valued the opportunity to maintain and develop their first languages, and confirmed the vital importance of bilingual support: 'The most helpful thing would be someone who can explain things in your first language.' One student, however pointed out that bilingual support needs to be equitably deployed, as bilingual support teachers may not always be able to help in multilingual classes: 'There was a bilingual teacher for the Asian students. We can't communicate with each other. I don't have any Ethiopian friends there.'

Some students on separate EAL provision commented on the social isolation sometimes associated with such provision and regretted that they had not been able to develop their communicative competence through contact with native speakers of English: 'In the Foundation group there were no native speakers to mix with. We didn't mix with other students in the school.' Others appreciated and clearly benefited from the specialist nature of good quality EAL provision in FE. This was particularly the case when students had had negative experiences in school:

Some teachers when they finished explaining to the class, they came to give you help. But others didn't. The geography teacher – he was very horrible to me – when I don't understand he used to get angry because he has to explain again and waste time. The first time I asked him he got angry and started shouting at me in class

– 'If you are listening you would understand!' I felt shy and I never asked him again.

Here [EAL Threshold Course in FE college] it is better than school. All students are the same level and don't laugh at each other. The teacher is good and always helps us and we are learning more English. The students are all friendly and help each other. We are like a family.

Continuity and progression

Interviewees highlighted difficulties associated with adapting to more informal and less didactic styles of teaching, and more active and independent styles of learning, than those they had been used to in their previous educational experience.

In Ethiopia we just listened to the teacher and took notes and then prepared for the exam. We never did homework assignments, or practicals in science, or presentations. The system here is really nice. I like it. You have to research, read books, understand more and develop your ideas.

It's a better way of learning. You do it yourself so you know what is wrong, and if you've done it yourself you're not going to forget. In my country even if you do homework you can just find the answer in the notes and that's it.

Here we do group work and practicals, and we have to research and use books in the library to find the answers. There, there was only the teacher and one text-book for the course, and that's it.

Students who had managed to adapt their learning style to new demands and to progress successfully within the system acknowledged three main factors which had helped them to do so – well-targeted language support, knowledge of the education system, and the acquisition of study skills.

Individually targeted language support linked to Communication Skills and Study Skills classes, and modes of study which combined individual research and investigative assignment work, such as some students experienced on courses like BTEC National, were identified as being a more effective preparation for higher education studies than unsupported A-Level study.

> I learned how to study and I understood the system of education well as a result of doing the BTEC National. If I had done A-Level I don't think I could have made the same progress. I have friends who were doing A Level at the same time. They still have problems with writing and they never really learned. They are good in their subjects but they couldn't get the university places they wanted. Some who are very good in maths are now doing a foundation course in university.

Another student who had done A-Levels confirmed this view: 'It was only in my second year at university that I got used to writing essays, using reference books, using the library. If I'd had more support at A-Level I could have done better.'

Those who had eventually succeeded in finding their way through the system the hard way – with minimal assistance – placed great importance upon knowledge of the system itself as being a prerequisite for effective choice and for finding the way through the complex system of qualifications. One account illustrates not only the complexity of the system which has to be negotiated, but also the pattern of repetition and low expectation which many bilingual students are condemned to, and the exceptional resilience and commitment that are required to emerge successfully from it:

> I am Eritrean and I completed my secondary education in Addis Ababa. English was the language of instruction in Ethiopia. I was studying science and maths and was interested in pharmacy. I came here at the age of 18. I joined an English course at an adult education institute and went there for three or four weeks in the mornings. It was very basic but at least I met some people. The teacher asked me why I was wasting my time there and suggested going to college. The next place I went to was a proper college, but it was too late to start because the science course was full. So I went to a general education course, but it was still too elementary – maths, English and very simple science. I stayed there for one year.

This country and the system was new to me so it was good to get to know about the system, but I wish if I knew someone who knows the country very well – which college, which courses. I could have done better if I had good advice. In that English course we were just filling in forms with our name and address. There was no homework. We were not fully assessed.

Another student reflected ruefully on her progress through the obstacle course, and on the profligate expense of time that an inadequately supported system demands:

I've managed to get what I wanted – I've got a degree. But it took me five or six years to find out about the system the hard way. Of course with the knowledge I now have – of the system and of what tutors expect – it would have been easier. I think I could have done it in two or three years if there had been good targeted support, especially in the A-level years.

Conclusion

The research examined the particular needs of refugee students, in both schools and colleges, in the context of the UK education system as it is currently developing. The recent and continuing changes in the structure and content of the education system, and especially in the post-16 qualifications framework, have raised important questions and stimulated a widening debate about the participation, progression and achievement of all students in the 14-19 cohort. The extent to which the system is able to meet the particular needs of refugee students is a valuable measure of its ability to deliver choice and entitlement to all students in concrete terms.

Ease of transition between other education systems and UK schools and colleges varied widely. Given lack of agreement and compatibility within the UK qualifications system itself, it is perhaps not surprising that there are particular difficulties in this country relating both to the lack of a system of equivalencies between UK and overseas qualifications and, more generally, to a lack of knowledge of other education systems. These difficulties are well known among adult refugees and others who seek recognition of overseas qualifications in this country.

They are less well known among young refugees seeking educational continuity as they enrol in UK schools and colleges.

However, despite these difficulties and barriers, some interviewees did manage an effective and relatively rapid transfer between education systems, and some progressed and achieved successfully in the UK system, although often at some personal cost and after considerable delays.

Factors which inhibited access and progress are manifold. Increasingly restrictive immigration and asylum legislation undermines international agreements on the rights of refugees, and exacerbates the conditions of insecurity and poverty in which refugees and asylum seekers try to re-establish their lives in this country. These conditions inevitably impact upon the educational prospects of young refugees and add to the barriers that confront them within the education system itself. Such barriers include lack of advice and guidance, difficulties in finding appropriate school and college places, inadequate initial assessment, a general shortage of EAL provision in FE, insufficient language and learning support in both schools and colleges, a lack of awareness of the situation of refugees on the part of some admissions and teaching staff, and a prevailing climate of low expectations and racist attitudes which seem to be as much structural as attitudinal features in some parts of the education system.

Clearly, in the brave new environment of the market place in education, the need for staff training in language and intercultural issues continues. At the same time, in a system which is tending towards increasing fragmentation in terms of curricular and institutional variation, coherent systems of information, advice and diagnostic assessment become ever more necessary, not least so that choice in education can retain some meaning. Accessible advice and guidance, strategically available at the point of entry into the system, and effective initial assessment, responsive to individual need and capable of accommodating – if not accrediting – previous educational experience in other education systems, would do much to obviate some of the waste of public resources and personal commitment caused by misdiagnosis of need and inappropriate placement.

If higher levels of participation and achievement are to become a reality, the needs and entitlements of all students will need to be met. The implementation of good practices which are designed to improve the quality of refugee students' education are likely to enhance the prospects of all students whose needs have not been sufficiently recognised.

Notes

1. This chapter is based on research carried out in 1994/5 which examined the educational experiences of young refugees who had attended schools and colleges in four London Boroughs. A report of the research, Entitled to Learn?, was published by the World University Service in 1995

2. The research sample only includes students who had made it into the education system. The experience of those who remain excluded from the system are only hinted at through the accounts of the difficulties encountered by those who achieved access.

3. For more details of this school's work with refugee students, c.f. Jones and Heilbronn, 1997.

CHAPTER TEN

The Educational Needs of Refugee Children

Crispin Jones

Introduction

This chapter looks at three main issues that emerged from investigations based in the International Centre for Intercultural Studies [ICIS] at the Institute of Education, into the educational needs of refugee students in inner London schools. The first are contextual and relate to the position of refugees, seen in their international, EU, UK and local frames of reference. The second is an examination of school based issues in primary and secondary schools and the third consists of suggestions for meeting the educational needs of refugee pupils more effectively.

Contextual issues

The 20th century could be said to be the century of the refugee. Its latter half has been marked by huge refugee movements across the world, many resulting from the long standing crisis in the notion of the state, with all its associated xenophobic and narrow nationalistic tendencies. More specifically, the illusion of the unitary, so-called 'nation state', with its associated concepts of insiders/citizens and outsiders and its denial of pluralism has led to the wholesale persecution of millions and the fleeing of even more people across national boundaries in search of refuge and asylum. Coupled with the post-1945 collapse of the European colonial empires, refugees have become a world-wide issue. The scale is staggering. Currently about 19 million refugees world-wide are recognised by the UNHCR, but such official statistics grossly underestimate the scale of the issue. There are another 25 million displaced people, most of whom are, to all intents and purposes, asylum seekers (Rutter, 1994).

Most people in Europe remain unaware of the huge numbers involved. The responsibility for looking after this vast number of people, including providing for their educational needs, does not fall on the states of the prosperous North. It is the poor countries of the South who provide sanctuary for the majority of refugees – over 80 per cent of them. The scale of this inequitable distribution is even more evident when one considers the ratio of refugees to population. In Britain, for example, the ratio is one refugee to 318 of the population: in Malawi it is one to nine and in Jordan, one to three (Refugee Council, 1993).

In European history, however, people seeking asylum have been a permanent feature, although schools within the EU seldom teach their students that this is so. For hundreds of years, Jews and Gypsies have been persecuted and chased across and out of Europe. The Second World War produced about sixty million refugees and displaced people, including some twenty million Germans. Moreover, the seeking of asylum in the European context is not simply a question of asylum-seekers entering or moving within Europe. It could be argued that the USA is an abiding monument to asylum seekers *from* Europe.

It is not just history, either. The collapse of the former Yugoslavia has produced well over three million refugees and displaced people, the majority of whom remain within the old borders of that state. By early 1996, about 320,000 had arrived in Germany, some 12,000 in Britain, although these figures are probably a considerable underestimate (Morrell, 1996). Nor are refugees from the former Yugoslavia the sole source of European refugees and there is every likelihood of more refugees from other parts of Europe entering the European Union during the next decade, particularly from states formerly under Soviet communist control.

This steady rise in the numbers of people seeking asylum in western Europe, coupled with the abolition of most of the EU's internal borders, has prompted a vigorous political debate on refugee policy in most EU states as well as in the central administration of the EU itself.

Although a harmonised approach to asylum and immigration law is emerging across the EU, the social rights of asylum-seekers and refugees still differ widely within the individual states. (This point is discussed in more detail in Chapter Two.) Harmonisation is important as it partially drives British government policy in this area. However, whatever the rights and wrongs of British government policy, the one sure fact is that numbers, internationally as well as in Europe, are likely to increase.

Narrowing the focus further, in Britain the vast majority of refugees and asylum-seekers are in London – some 90 per cent of them. It is difficult to be precise because of the lack of accurate data: for example, estimates of the refugee and asylum seeking population of one London borough in 1994 ranged from 5,000-15,000. Keeping in mind that variation, in May 1997 it was estimated by the Refugee Council that there were approximately 39,000 refugee pupils in Greater London (Refugee Council, 1997) and that number has probably increased since. In practice, these figures mean that nearly every school in inner London has refugee pupils, and some have large numbers. Yet local authorities in London have to deal with an increasing range of refugee needs while their resource base continued to shrink.

Despite the dwindling resource base, many London local authorities are concerned about the level of service that they provide to refugees and asylum seekers. Consultations and conferences in numerous of London boroughs over the last few years reveal a range of issues that impact upon the lives of asylum seekers and refugees and which clearly impact upon education. Among the most significant are the following.

*   *Information issues*: There is a need for good, accurate and relevant information, including statistical data, to be collected, so that all local services can be made more effective. Some of this information should also be available in the languages of the major refugee communities, to help them to meet their immediate and long term needs. The collection and dissemination of such information also has clear implications for staff development within institutions, to ensure that the information is used in a productive manner. In particular, full statistical and background information in relation to refugee pupils is crucial for effective school policies.

- *Administration issues*: A more effective, integrated, multi-agency approach to refugee issues is clearly needed. This has two aspects: firstly, better and more senior co-ordination within the concerned agencies and between them and refugee community groups; secondly, more accessible multi-agency help and information points for refugees. The educational needs of refugee pupils, for example, cannot easily be divorced from other out of school issues faced by many refugee families and/or individuals. Schools sometimes do become the key information point for refugees but seldom have the expertise to deal with the range of issues involved.

- *Recognition of the strengths within refugee communities*: Much current provision does little to prevent the wastage of existing talent in refugee communities, particularly among women. For example, there is a need for more funded refugee advice and advocacy centres, refugee managed, to help refugees understand and use the services available to them. Such centres would also help build up expertise within the refugee communities in relation to dealings with public services, including schools and LEAs.

- *Interpreting and translation issues*: While the valuable work done by the various translation services is acknowledged, there is general agreement across London that they need to be expanded – not specifically for refugees but more generally for multilingual London. Translation services are also an educational need, which current school budgets find difficult to meet.

- *Racism/discrimination/xenophobia*: More effective action is urgently required concerning the racial harassment of refugees and asylum seekers. Official agencies are needed to give a moral lead, both by welcoming refugees and supporting initiatives to combat racism. Again, these issues are not exclusive to refugees. However, a great deal of work remains for schools to do in relation to this complex issue, and there is some helpful research which indicates ways forward (CME, 1992a; Hewitt, 1996; Kahin, 1997).

- *Financial issues*: In a time of continuing budget cuts, it can be argued that clearer priorities and objectives might ensure that the existing finance is used more effectively. The way in which the education system has relied on Section 11 to fund EAL teaching is a case in point. Designed as transition funding, to enable LEAs to reorder their financial priorities in relation to EAL work, it has been retained because of the need but also because budgets have not been re-prioritised.

- *Accountability*: There continues to be much discussion about more public accountability in relation to public provision for refugees and asylum-seekers. This is at all levels of service, from central government downwards; in educational terms, it refers to the DfEE and OFSTED as well as to individual LEAs and schools.

- *Educational issues*: In the range of consultations, education always comes up, although perhaps not as the central issue that many in education see it as being. Better access to appropriate education is often argued, especially in relation to language teaching. This is needed for the whole refugee age range, from pre-school to adult and further education. Access to basic education, including English language must be available to all refugees who want it. In relation to children in school, the most frequent request is for more council interpreters to be available to schools to help improve school/refugee community links. The need for more child care provision for refugee women who want to go to college [or, indeed, to work] is also considered important. However, the range of issues identified all have implications for education.

School based issues

The investigations by the International Centre for Intercultural Studies (ICIS) over the last six years have been into both primary and secondary schools in inner London. In the primary school study, undertaken in the London Borough of Greenwich, the borough's Central Race Equality Unit co-ordinated a series of meetings about the educational needs of refugees, in which the range of concerned agencies from within the London Borough of Greenwich discussed potential research areas with the ICIS. A wide range of issues was identified but it was decided to concentrate on on, given the resources available. A detailed investigation of refugee children in primary schools was decided upon, with the intention that the enquiry would come up with more detailed information about the educational difficulties that such children might face in school and, equally importantly, with realistic recommendations for schools that would enable them to meet the educational needs of their refugee children more adequately.

The procedure adopted was to make a detailed examination of practice in one primary school in the borough. From such a detailed study, it was hoped, would come insights into refugee children's educational needs that a large scale survey might not reveal. It was also stressed that any recommendations that arose from the work would have to be realistic in terms of resources, given the straitened circumstances of many of the schools in Greenwich and indeed, across the country.

ICIS was lucky to obtain the services of Lynda Miller, a child psycho-therapist, to undertake the research. A number of primary schools with significant numbers of refugees were identified and the researcher chose the second one she visited. The details that follow are based on her research (LBG, 1994).

Over a two term study, six areas for further investigation emerged. These were:

- *Language related issues*: Chiefly, these related to EAL, parti-cularly the failure to meet the bilingual needs of refugee pupils.

- *Relevance of background information*: Teachers in the school wished to know more about the background of their refugee pupils than they did – such as countries from which their refugee pupils came, details about history, language(s) and religion(s), the school-ing system there and the reasons that have led people to flee and seek asylum in Britain.

- *Limited communication with families*: Although partly a language issue, the teachers also felt that there was less communication with parents than there should have been.

- *Difficulty in developing community links*: The teachers knew about local refugee community organisations but had yet to make contact with them, even though they felt that such contact would be beneficial.

- *Emotional and behavioural issues*: The teachers were aware that some of the refugee pupils had had traumatic experiences. They felt ill-equipped to deal with this and wanted more information about what to do and who to turn to for help when issues relating to trauma arose.

- *Identified needs in context of overall demands on teachers' time*: The demands on teachers' time in primary schools are constantly increasing. While accepting that refugee pupils' educational needs did have a priority, the teachers did not see where they could find the time (and energy) to deal with them adequately.

The interesting thing about this list is that it contains few surprises. The points raised were not dissimilar to those raised by refugee communities themselves in the various consultation exercises that have taken place elsewhere in London. However, such lists both help to clarify the issues and help in drawing up priorities for action, particularly when schools find themselves short of resources, a point that will be taken up later in the chapter.

The work in secondary schools has been over a longer period and has involved work in a range of inner London comprehensive schools. In our opening chapter, Jill Rutter and I discussed the issue of the myth of the failing secondary school and the refugee student. We concluded that refugee students are not a problem and they do not all attend failing schools – however such failure is defined. More, their presence in schools is not detrimental to that school's performance, however measured. We indicated the positive impact that refugees have made on British society over the years. Without them, British society would be the poorer in every sense of the word.

The research in general confirmed these points. However, it also revealed that issues that trouble education in inner London are foregrounded by the presence of refugee students. Again, it is useful to list the major issues arising from the investigation, and to compare them with the issues it identified.

- *Teaching about refugee issues to non-refugee children*: Many of the refugee students in the secondary schools studied were subjected to prejudice and discrimination, as no doubt they do in other secondary schools and in the wider society generally. Among many of the non-refugee pupils interviewed, there was superficial acceptance of refugee pupils but underneath there was quite a lot of hostility, some outright racism and a considerable amount of wearied acceptance on both sides. However, it was encouraging to find that, in most cases, the schools' pro-refugee stance was accepted by the students and that those expressing strong anti-refugee feelings were generally met with disapproval. In addition, much of the negative feeling seemed to be more anti-newcomer than anti-Black or anti-refugee. And even that is too simple, as inter-group relations among young people in London appear to be moving towards more complex alignments (Hewitt, 1996).

- *Language issues relating to the teaching of English and development of students' first (and sometimes second) languages*: As in the primary study, teachers in the secondary schools studied frequently felt that the EAL support they could give was very inadequate. Given the large number of bilingual pupils in the schools of London and the relatively poor funding for this crucial area of work, it is not surprising that refugee pupils frequently do not get the language support they need. This is not just an issue about English. Support for the development of the first language of refugee children in mainstream school was almost non-existent and consequently remains a major task for local community supplementary schools and classes.

- *Giving appropriate emotional and pastoral support*: includes but goes beyond the issue of trauma. For example, there were significant numbers of unaccompanied refugee young people in the studied schools and they frequently required support to help cope with their often difficult situations. Nearly all had required support at some time and that support was often more than emotional. Some needed advice about housing, health and various legal issues relating to their status. The schools with large numbers of refugee pupils had frequently built up an *ad hoc* expertise in giving such advice and support but it was seldom systematic.

- *The dangers of stereotyping refugee children*: This issue links in with the previous one. Not all refugees are traumatised, although there are many who are. Nor are they 'educational problems' or 'failures' as sometimes labelled. Indeed, in a very real sense, refugee students were seen by many of their teachers as enriching the schools they attended. Many appeared eager to use their schooling to their best of their abilities and the schools accepted and tried to ensure that this was both recognised and supported. That some teachers have low expectations of their pupils, including refugees has been long recognised as a common fault in many inner city schools (e.g. DES, 1980). Although this was picked up in some of the conversations with teachers in relation to the refugees, it should be emphasised that this was notably infrequent.

- *'Yet another task....' resource issues*: Teachers in inner city comprehensive schools have always been stretched. The range of extra educational issues they have to deal with is very extensive. Some of the teachers in the schools studied did indeed see refugees as the last straw for their camel-like backs, but most did not, Refugee pupils do present real resource issues to schools, however: the cosmetic changes in Section 11 eligibility, which have extended mainly language related funding to refugee pupils without increasing the global sums available, mean that the schools still desperately need more resources to deal effectively with the issues that the refugee presence raised. And one question remains uninvestigated: What is the effect of the balance that each school placed on pastoral and academic issues, however crudely defined? Does the time [a finite resource] put into pastoral care detract from academic care and subsequent academic performance and vice versa?

- *Home/school community links*: This was a complex issue, with no two of the schools facing similar issues. The schools had strong links with some of the communities they served, weak links with others and non-existent or even negative links with yet others. Negative links were often related to more general racial tensions in the area (CME, 1992; Hewitt, 1996).

- *Consistency of approach*: In all the schools studied, issues of refugee education tied in with broader issues of pedagogic consistency in the school, particularly dealing with racism and the issue of expectations – some teachers do have low expectations of pupils and some children have unjustified low expectations of themselves.

- *Mid-term admissions and induction policies*: This was identified as being important and most of the schools had developed or were developing strategies to deal with all that it entailed. This is discussed elsewhere in the book, particularly in Caroline Lodge's chapter. A good induction for a new arrival was considered to be a crucial element in the successful education of refugee pupils. Failure to provide it was thought to be a considerable obstacle to their educational careers.

Like the primary schools, the secondary schools generally felt that there was much more that could be done with refugee students and that that improvement tied in with more general issues of school improvement. Most of the schools studied, despite being short of resources, were willing to re-distribute what they had to enhance the quality of the education provided for their refugees. I shall sum up he most significant and readily implemented approaches and strategies for improving the education of refugee children in schools that emerged from the investigation.

- *Refugee students should be seen as an integral part of the education system, not a 'problem'*. This was widely seen as an essential first step, although it proved surprisingly difficult to put into practice. It does not mean that teachers should be insensitive to the needs of refugee students but rather that they should be seen as a normal part of the educational system, like other groups such as bilingual students, the talented and gifted, ethnic minority students and students with special educational needs.

- *Barriers to curriculum access should be identified and then overcome*. The wide range of practices affecting curricular access need to be better identified and tackled – as discussed in other chapters of this book.

- *Information and resources should be collated and distributed*. Teachers still need more information about educating refugee children. At its most simple, this would include providing basic factual data, such as home country profiles, similar to those found in Jill Rutter's excellent *Refugee Children in the Classroom* (1994).

- *Community resources should be identifed and harnessed.* With greater use of refugee community resources could be made by just about all schools.

- *Linguistic resources should be made available.* Not only EAL and translation services but also mother tongues require attention. This applies to all bilingual students, but newly arrived refugee students are even less likely to have access to the range of support classes enjoyed by other, more established bilingual groups.

- *School induction should be appropriate.* Many schools that have significant numbers of refugee students have developed excellent induction policies to ease their entry into the school but their are others which still need to put policies in place to accommodate refugee students.

- *Provide appropriate support for traumatised pupils.* Some refugee students will need more extensive support than can be provided by the normal pastoral system of schools. The expertise is available (see Chapters Five and Seven) but its use has resource implications which should not fall upon a school's already stretched budget.

- *Provide effective academic and pastoral support for refugee pupils and their teachers.* This links in with the last point. What is important is that it applies to both teachers and their refugee students.

- *Teachers need in-service training to teach against prejudice generally and to respond to the educational needs of refugees.* Anti-racist policies are still regarded as important in many inner London schools. What is still needed, however, is greater understanding of the curricular and pedagogic implications of such policies. In specific relation to refugees, there is still very little good practice to disseminate.

- Criteria of success should be identified and monitored. Finally, policies are useless if no criteria for success are established and no monitoring systems set up to assess the success or failure of the institution in relation to the set criteria. Learning from our mistakes and our successes is important.

Such recommendations will be familiar to those concerned with the more effective education of refugee students. However, the work undertaken by the ICIS is ongoing, mainly through the Refugee Education Initiative. Finding out about the issues has been comparatively easy. Developing the policies and practice to deal with the range of issues will take longer and be more difficult. Given the range of pressures on inner city schools at the moment, the wonder is that so much has been done in some schools. However, much more remains to be done before all refugee students can receive the educational entitlement that is their right.

Bibliography

Ajdukovic, M., and Ajdukovic, D. (1992) 'Psychological well-being of refugee children' *Child Abuse and Neglect*, Vol. 17, pp 843 – 854

Aldrich, G.H. and van Baarda, Th.A. (1994) *Declaration of Amsterdam – the Declaration and Recommendations on the Rights of Children in Armed Conflict* The Hague: International Dialogues Foundation

American Psychiatric Association (1980) *Diagnostic and Statistical Manual of Mental Disorders* (third edition) Washington, DC: APA

American Psychiatric Association (1994) *Diagnostic and Statistical Manual of Mental Disorders* (fourth edition). Washington, DC: APA

Ayalon, O. (1983) 'Coping with terrorism: The Israeli case' in Meichenbaum, D. and Jaremko, M. (eds) *Stress Reduction and Prevention* New York: Plenum. pp. 293-339

Ayalon, O. (1988) *Rescue! Community Oriented Preventive Education for Coping with Stress* Haifa: Nord Publications

Baily, R. (1995) *Survivors with hidden scars: the mediating role of the school in helping refugee children integrate their experiences and make the transition to life in the host society* M.A. dissertation, Department of Peace Studies, University of Bradford

Baines, S. (1994) 'The Mafalda Nursery' *Nursery World*, 94:3430, pp 14-15

Baker, R. (1983) 'Refugees: an overview of an international problem' in Baker, R. (Ed) *The Psychosocial Problems of Refugees* London: The British Refugee Council

Barnet Borough Voluntary Services Council (1995) *Refugees in Barnet* London: BBVSC.

Bash, L. *et al.* (1984) *Urban Schooling: Theory and Practice* London: Holt, Rinehart and Winston.

Bash, L. (1995) 'The integration of youth in the UK: the case of the Jewish community' in Bash, L. and Green, A. (Ed), *The World Yearbook of Education 1995. Youth, Education and Work* London: Kogan Page

Bell, A. (1996) *Only for Three Months: the Basque Children in Exile* Norwich: Mousehole Press

Bellamy, C. (1996) 'The end of war – and peace.' *The Independent*, 14 June, 1996, p. 1

Biehal, N., Clayden, J., Stein, M. and Wade, J. (1992) *Prepared for Living?* London: National Children's Bureau

Bloch, A. (1994) *Refugees and Migrants in Newham* London: University of East London.

Blom, G. (1986) 'A school disaster – intervention and research aspects.' *Journal of the American Academy of Child Psychiatry*, 25, pp 336-345

Boyden, J. and Hudson, A.. (1985) *Children: Rights and Responsibilities*, London: Minority Rights Group

BRC. (British Refugee Council) (1993) *Who is a Refugee?* London: Refugee Council

Brent, London Borough of (1993) *Refugees in Brent*. London: LB Brent Policy Unit

Brown, C. (1995) 'Children sent alone to seek asylum in UK' *The Independent*, 4 December, 1995, p 1

Burke, J., Borus, J., Burns, B., Millstein, K. and Beasley, M. (1982) 'Changes in children's behaviour after a natural disaster.' *American Journal of Psychiatry*, 139, pp 1010-1014

Burke, J., Moccia, P., Borus, J. and Burns, B.(1986) 'Emotional distress in fifth-grade children ten months after a natural disaster' *Journal of the American Academy of Child Psychiatry*, 25, 536-541

Butler, L. and Lloyd, R. (1994) *Homeless in the 1990s: Local Authority Practice*. London: Shelter

Carbarino, J. (1993) 'Challenges we face in understanding children and war: a personal essay' *Child Abuse and Neglect*, Vol 17, pp 787 -793

Carey-Wood, J., Marshall, T., (1995) *The Settlement of Refugees in Britain. Home Office Study No 41* London: HMSO/Home Office Research and Planning Unit

Carter, M. (1995) *Out of Sight... London's Continuing B and B Crisis* London: South Bank University and London Homelessness Forum

Christian Aid (1996) *Aid Statistics* London: Christian Aid

Clarke, P. and Millikan, J. (1986) *Developing Multi-cultural Perspectives* Richmond, Australia: Richmond Multi-cultural Resource Centre

Cooper, G. (1994) 'Buddy' system aids school to ease pain of pupils in exile' *The Independent*, 27 October, 1994, p 9

CME. [Centre for Multicultural Education] (1992) *Sagaland: Youth Culture, Racism and Education: A Report on Research Carried out in Thamesmead*. London: London Borough of Greenwich

CME [Centre for Multicultural Education] (1994) *The Needs of Refugee Children in Primary School*. Unpublished research project undertaken by the Centre for Multicultural Education, Institute of Education, London University on behalf of the Central Race Equality Unit, London Borough of Greenwich.

Crane, H. (1990) *Speaking from Experience – working with homeless families*. London: Bayswater Hotel Homeless Project

Daly, E. (1997) 'No peace for the war babies' *The Independent Tabloid*, 19 February, 1997, pp 2 -3

Department of Health/OFSTED (1995) *The Education of Children who are Looked After by Local Authorities*, London: HMSO

Department of Health Social Services Inspectorate (1995a) *Unaccompanied Asylum-seeking Children: A Practice Guide*. London: HMSO

Department of Health Social Services Inspectorate (1995b) *Unaccompanied Asylum-seeking Children: A Training Pack*, London: HMSO

DES [Dept. of Education and Science] (1980) *Report by HM Inspectors on Educational Provision by the Inner London Education Authority*, Summer 1980 London, DES.

DFE (1993) *The Charter for Further Education*. London: DFE

DFE (1994) *Our Children's Education – The Updated Parents' Charter.* London: DFE

Education Development Centre. (1996) *Making it Real: Introducing a Global Dimension in the Early Years*, London: Education Development Centre and Save the Children

DHSS (1980) *Inequalities in Health: a Report of a Research Working Group* (The Black Report) London: DHSS

Duckworth, D. (1986) 'Psychological problems arising from disaster work'. *Stress Medicine*, 2, pp 315-323

Dyregrov, A. (1988) *Critical incident stress debriefings*. Unpublished manuscript, Research Centre for Occupational Health and Safety, University of Bergen, Norway

Dyregrov, A. (1991) *Grief in Children: A Handbook for Adults*. London: Jessica Kingsley Publishers

Edwards, R., (1992) 'Co-ordination, Fragmentation and Definitions of Need: the new under fives initiative and homeless families' *Children and Society*, 6 (4) pp 336-352

Edwards, V. (1995) *Speaking and Listening in Multilingual Classrooms* Reading: University of Reading Reading and Language Information Centre

Elbedour, S., ten Bensel, R. and Bastien, D. (1993) 'Ecological integrated model of children of war: Individual and social psychology' *Child Abuse and Neglect*, 17, pp 805-819

Farberow, N. and Gordon, N. (1981) *Manual for Child Health Workers in Major Disasters*. Washington, DC: U.S. Government Printing Office, DHHS Publication No. (ADM 81-1070)

Feingold, J. *et al* (1990) *A British Baccalaureate*. London: Institute for Public Policy Research

Fethney, M. (1990) *The Absurd and the Brave* Lewes: Book Guild

Finlay, R. (1990) *Unaccompanied Refugee Children: A Monitoring Report* London: Refugee Council

Frederick, C. (1985). 'Children traumatised by catastrophic situations' in Eth, S. and. Pynoos, R. (Eds) *Post-Traumatic Stress Disorder in Children* Washington: American Psychiatric Press, pp 7399

Furley, A. (1989) *A Bad Start in Life – Children, Health and Housing* London: Shelter

Further Education Funding Council (FEFC) (1995) *Schedule Two, Further and Higher Education Act 1994* London: FEFC

Galante, R., and Foa, D. (1986) 'An epidemiological study of psychic trauma and treatment effectiveness after a natural disaster' *Journal of the American Academy of Child Psychiatry*, 25, 357363

George Orwell School (1993) *Safe in Another Country* Video programme by George Orwell School, Islington, London

Gewirtz, S., Ball, S., and Bowe, R. (1995) *Markets, Choice and Equity in Education* Buckingham: Open University

Gershon, K. (ed) (1989) *We Came as Children*, London and Basingstoke: Papermac/Macmillan

Gibbs, M. (1989) 'Factors in the victim that mediate between disaster and psychopathology: A review.' *Journal of Traumatic Stress*, 2, 489-514

Gillis, H. (1993) 'Individual and small-group psychotherapy for children involved in trauma and disaster' in Saylor, C. (Ed) *Children and Disasters* New York: Plenum. pp 165-186

Halliday, G. (1987) 'Direct psychological therapies for nightmares: a review.' *Clinical Psychology Review*, 7, 501-523

Harris, A. and Hewitt, M. (1990) *Talking Time*. London: Learning by Design

Hewitt, R. (1996) *Routes of Racism* Stoke-on-Trent: Trentham Books

Hjern, A., Angel, B. and Hbjer, B. (1991) 'Persecution and behaviour: a report of refugee children in Chile' *Child Abuse and Neglect*, Vol. 15, pp 239-248

HMI (1993) *Educational Support for Minority Ethnic Communities* London: HMSO

HMI (1990) *A Survey of the Education of Children Living in Temporary Accommodation.* London: DES

Home Office (1995) *Asylum Statistics*, 1985-95. London: Home Office Statistical Department

Home Office (1996) *Unpublished Quarterly Asylum Statistics*, January-June 1996. London: Home Office Statistical Department

Horowitz, M. (1976) *Stress-response syndromes* New York: Jason Aronson

Horowitz, M. Wilner, N., and Alvarez, W. (1979). 'Impact of event scale: A measure of subjective stress.' *Psychosomatic Medicine*, 41, pp 209218

Howarth, V. (1987) *Survey of Families in Bed and Breakfast Hotels.* London: Thomas Coram Foundation for Children

Hyder, T. (1996) 'Helping children from refugee families', *Co-ordinate*, 52 pp 6-8

Kendrick, P., Ryan, V., Wilson, K. (1992) *Play Therapy: A Non-directive Approach for Children and Adolescents,* London: Bailliere Tindall

ILEA (1987) *Homeless families: Implications for Educational Provision* London: ILEA

International Broadcasting Trust (1992) *The Dispossessed: an action video pack* London: IBT

IOE/MORI (1995) *English Language Needs Amongst Linguistic Minority Adults in England and Wales* (Draft final report for Adult Basic Skills Literacy Unit London: IOE/MORI

Janoff-Bulman, R. (1985) 'The aftermath of victimisation: Rebuilding shattered assumptions' in Figley, C. (Ed) *Trauma and its Wake*. Vol.1 New York: Brunner/Mazel

Jackson, S. (1988) *The Education of Children in Care* [Bristol Papers No 1] Bristol: University of Bristol School of Applied Social Services

Johnson, K. (1993) *School crisis management: A Team Training Guide* Alameda, CA: Hunter House

Jencks, C.(1994) *The Homeless* Cambridge, Mass.: Harvard University Press

Jewett, C. (1993) *Helping Children Cope with Separation and Loss* London: Batsford.

Jockenhövel-Schieke, H. (Ed) (1990) *Unaccompanied Refugee Children in Europe: Experience with Protection, Placement and Education* Frankfurt/Main: International Social Service German Branch, p 192

Jones, C. (1993) 'Refugee children in English urban schools' *European Journal of Intercultural Studies*, 3 (2/3), pp 29-40

Jones, C. and Heilbronn, R. (Eds) (1997) *New Teachers in an Urban Comprehensive: Learning in Partnership* School Stoke-on-Trent: Trentham Books

Jones, T. (1993) *Britain's Ethnic Minorities* London: Policy Studies Institute

Keppel-Benson, J. and Ollendick, T. (1993) 'Post traumatic stress disorders in children and adolescents.' In Saylor, C. (Ed) *Children and Disasters.* New York: Plenum. pp 29-43

Klein, G. (1993) *Education Towards Race Equality.* London: Cassell

Klein, R. (1995) 'Services with a smile' *Times Educational Supplement*, 13 October, 1996.

Klingman, A. (1993) 'School-based intervention following a disaster' in Saylor. C. F. (Ed) *Children and Disasters.* New York: Plenum. pp 187-210

Kuebli ,J. (1994) 'Young children's understanding of everyday emotions' *Young Children*, 49:3 pp 36-47

LBG [London Borough of Greenwich Central Race Equality Unit] (1994a) *Refugee Communities and Local Authority Provision* [Unpublished conference report for the London Borough of Greenwich]

LBG [London Borough of Greenwich Race Equality Unit] (1994b) *Summary Report: The Educational Needs of Refugee Children in Primary Schools* London: London Borough of Greenwich Race Equality Unit

Levine, J. (ed) (1990) *Bilingual learners and the mainstream curriculum* Basingstoke: The Falmer Press

Lodge, C. (1992). 'Integrating pupils who speak no English' *Pastoral Care in Education*, 10 (2), 3235

Lodge, C. (1995). 'Working with Refugees in Schools' *Pastoral Care in Education*, 13 (2), 1113

London, L. (1989) British Government Policy and Jewish Refugees *Patterns of Prejudice*, Vol 23, no 4, p 30

Lonigan, C., Shannon, M., Finch, A., Daugherty, T. and Saylor, C. (1991) 'Children's reactions to a natural disaster: Symptom severity and degree of exposure' *Advances in Behaviour Research and Therapy,* 13, 135-154

Lynch, E. and Hanson, M. (1992) *Developing Cross-cultural Competence: a Guide for Working with Young Children and Their Families* London: Paul Brookes

Magwaza, A., Killan, B., Peterson, I. and Pillay, Y. 'The effects of chronic violence on pre-school children living in South African Townships' *Child Abuse and Neglect*, Vol. 17 pp 795 – 803

McFarlane, A. (1987). 'Family functioning and overprotection following a natural disaster: The longitudinal effects of posttraumatic morbidity' *Australia and New Zealand Journal of Psychiatry*, 21, 210218

McFarlane, A., Policansky, S. and Irwin, C. (1987).' A longitudinal study of the psychological morbidity in children due to a natural disaster' *Psychological Medicine*, 17, 727738

Marks, I. (1978) 'Rehearsal relief of a nightmare' *British Journal of Psychiatry*, 133, 461-465

Martin, S. and Little, B. (1986) 'The effects of a natural disaster on academic abilities and social behaviour of school children' *British Columbia Journal of Special Education*, 10, 167-182

Meichenbaum, D. (1975) 'Self instructional methods.' In Kanfer, F. and Goldstein, A.. (eds) *Helping People* Change New York: Pergamon. pp 357-391

Meichenbaum, D. and Cameron, R. (1983) 'Stress inoculation training: toward a general paradigm for training coping skills' In Meichenbaum D. and Jaremko. M. (eds) *Stress Reduction and Prevention* New York: Plenum pp 115-154

Melzak, S. (nd) *Thinking about the internal and external experiences of refugee children in Europe, conflict and treatment* Unpublished paper

Melzak, S. and Warner, R. (1992) *Integrating Refugee Children into Schools* London: Medical Foundation/Minority Rights Group

Milgram, R. and Milgram, N. (1976) 'The effects of the Yom Kippur war on anxiety level in Israeli children' *Journal of Psychology*, 94, 107-113

Miller, K. (1992) 'Guidelines for helping non-English speaking children adjust and communicate' in Neugebauer, B. (Ed) *Alike and Different: Exploring our Humanity with Young Children* Washington DC: NAEYC

Milner, D. (1983) *Children and Race: Ten Years On* London: Ward Lock Educational

Misch, P., Phillips, M., Evans, P. and Berelowitz, M. (1993) 'Trauma in pre-school children: A clinical account' In Forrest, G. (Ed) *Trauma and Crisis Management.* ACPP Occasional Paper

Morrell, C. (1996) 'Refugee course to stay' *The Times Educational Supplement* 23 February 1996, p 15

Morton, S. (1988) *Homeless Families in Manchester* Manchester: Faculty of Community Medicine, University of Manchester

Mougne, C. (1985) *Vietnamese Children's Home: A Special Case for Care?* London: Save the Children, p 17

Murie, A. and Jeffers, S. (1987) *Living in Bed and Breakfast: the Experience of Homelessness in London* Bristol: School of Advanced Urban Studies

Nader, K., Pynoos, R., Fairbanks, L. and Frederick, C. (1991) 'Childhood PTSD Reactions one year after a sniper attack' *American Journal of Psychiatry,* 147, pp 1526-1530

National Children's Bureau (1987) *Investing in the Future – child health ten years after the Court Report.* London: National Children's Bureau

Newham Council Education Department (1996) *Guidelines on Whole-school Language Policies and Bilingual English Learners* London: L. B. Newham

Newman, C. (1976) 'Children of disaster: Clinical observation at Buffalo Creek' *American Journal of Psychiatry,* 133, pp 306-312

O'Donohue, W. and Eliot, A. (1992)'The current status of post traumatic stress syndrome as a diagnostic category: problems and proposals.' *Journal of Traumatic Stress*, 5, pp 421-439

Palace, E.and Johnston, C. (1989) 'Treatment of recurrent nightmares by the dream reorganisation approach' *Journal of Behaviour Therapy and Experimental Psychiatry*, 20, pp 219-226

Parry Jones, W (1992) *Children of Lockerbie* Paper presented at Guys Hospital meeting

Pereira, D. and Richman, N. (1991) *Helping children in difficult circumstances* London: Save the Children

Pollard, A. and Filer. A. (1966) *The Social World of Children's Learning: case Studies from Four to Seven* London: Cassell

Power, S., Whitty, G. and Youdell, D. (1995) *No Place to Learn: Homelessness and Education.* London: Shelter

Pynoos, R.and Eth, S. (1986) 'Witness to violence: the child interview.' *Journal of the American Academy of Child Psychiatry,* 25, 306-319

Pynoos, R. Frederick, C., Nader, K., Arroyo, W., Steinberg, A., Eth, S., Nunez, F. and Fairbanks, L. (1987). 'Life threat and post-traumatic stress in schoolage children' *Archives of General Psychiatry*, 44, 10571063

Pynoos, R., Goenjian, A., Karakashian, M., Tashjian, M., Manjikian, R., Manoukian, G., Steinberg, A. and Fairbanks, L.A. (1993) 'Post-traumatic stress reactions in children after the 1988 Armenian earthquake' *British Journal of Psychiatry*, 163, 239-247

Pynoos, R. and Nader, K. (1988) 'Psychological first aid and treatment approach for children exposed to community violence: research implications' *Journal of Traumatic Stress*, 1, 243-267

Rachman, S. (1980) 'Emotional processing.' *Behaviour Research and Therapy,* 18, 5160.

Refugee Council, Save the Children Fund, Ockenden Venture and Refugee Action (unpublished report, February 1984) *Unaccompanied Refugee Minors in the United Kingdom*

Refugee Council (1994a) 'Changes to Access to Housing for Asylum-Seekers', *RASU Bulletin*, London: Refugee Council

Refugee Council. (1994b) *Refugee Children in Schools.* London: Refugee Council

Refugee Council (1996a) *Asylum and Immigration Act 1996: a Factfile.* London: Refugee Council

Refugee Council (1997) *Refugee Children in School* (Unpublished Statistics)

Refugee Council and Save the Children (1996) *No Refuge for Children* London: Refugee Council and Save the Children

Ressler, E. M., Boothby, N. and Steinbock, D. J. (1988) *Unaccompanied Children* New York and Oxford: OUP, p 4

Richards, D. and Lovell, K. (1990) *Imaginal and in-vivo exposure in the treatment of PTSD* Paper read at Second European Conference on Traumatic Stress, Netherlands, September 1990

Richards, D. and Rose, J. (1991) 'Exposure therapy for post-traumatic stress disorder: Four case studies' *British Journal of Psychiatry,* 158, 836-840.

Richman, N. (1993a) *Communicating with Children: Helping Children in Distress. Development Manual 2* London: Save the Children

Richman, N. (1993b) 'Annotation: children in situations of political violence' *Journal of Child Psychology and Psychiatry*, Vol 34, No.8, pp 1286 -1302

Richman, N. (1998) *In the Midst of a Whirlwind: a Manual on Working with Refugee Children and Their Families* Stoke-on-Trent: Trentham Books

Robinson, R. and Mitchell, J. (1993) 'Evaluation of psychological debriefings' *Journal of Traumatic Stress*, 6, 367-382

Rutter, M. (1985) 'Resilience in the Face of Adversity – Protective Factors and Resistance to Psychiatric Disorder' in *British Journal of Psychiatry*, 147, pp 598-611

Rutter, J. (1991, 2nd ed 1996). *We left because we had to: an educational book for 14-18 year olds* London: Refugee Council

Rutter, J. (1992) *Refugees: a resource book for 8-13 year olds* London: Refugee Council

Rutter, J. (1994) *Refugee Children in the Classroom* Stoke-on Trent: Trentham Books

Rutter, J. (1997) 'Working with Refugee Children and their Families.' In Bastiani, J. (ed) (1997) *Home-School Work in Multicultural Settings.* London: David Fulton Publishers

Saigh, P. A. (1986). 'In vitro flooding in the treatment of a 6yrold boy's post-traumatic stress disorder.' *Behaviour Research and Therapy*, 24, 685688

Saigh, P.A. (1992) 'The behavioural treatment of child and adolescent posttraumatic stress disorder.' *Advances in Behaviour Research and Therapy*, 14, 247-275

Seligman, M. E. and Yellen, A. (1987) 'What is a dream?' *Behaviour Research and Therapy*, 25, pp 1-24

Sharma, R. (1987) *No Place Like Home: A Report by the West London Homelessness Group.* London: West London Homelessness Group

Shelter (1995) *No Place to Learn – Homelessness and Education* London: Shelter.

Sherriff, C. (Ed) (1995) *Reaching First Base: Guidelines of Good Practice on Meeting the Needs of Refugee Children from the Horn of Africa* London: Day-care Trust

Silver, N. (1995) *The Death of Yugoslavia.* London: BBC Books

Siraj Blatchford, I. (1994) *The Early Years: Laying the Foundations for Racial Equality*, Stoke-on-Trent: Trentham Books

Smith, M. and Noble, S. (1995) *Education Divides, Poverty and Schooling in the 1990s.* London: Child Poverty Action Group

Smith, M. and Noble, S. (1995) *Education Divides, Poverty and Schooling in the 1990s* London: Child Poverty Action Group

Spafford, T. and Bolloten, B. (1995) 'The admission and induction of refugee children into school' in *Multicultural Teaching*, Vol. 14, No. 1. pp 7-10.

Sparks, L. (1989) *Anti-Bias Curriculum: Tools for Empowering Young Children*, Washington DC: National Association for the Education of Young Children

Stallard, P. and Law, F. (1993) 'Screening and psychological debriefing of adolescent survivors of life-threatening events' *British Journal of Psychiatry*, 163, pp 660-665

Statler, J. (1990) *Special Relations.* London: Imperial War Museum

Stearns, S. D. (1993) 'Psychological distress and relief work: who helps the helpers' *Refugee Participation Network*, 15, pp 3-8

Sullivan, M.A., Saylor, C.F. and Foster, K.Y. (1991) 'Post-hurricane adjustment of pre-schoolers and their families' *Advances in Behaviour Research and Therapy*, 13, pp 163-171

Tang, M. (1994) *Vietnamese Refugees – Towards a Healthy Future* London: Deptford Vietnamese Health Project

Terr, L.C. (1988) 'What happens to early memories of trauma? A study of twenty children under age five at the time of documented traumatic events.' *Journal of the American Academy of Child and Adolescent Psychiatry*, 27, pp 96-104

Tsui, E., Dagwell, K. and Yule, W. (in preparation) *Effect of a disaster on children's academic attainment*

United Nations High Commissioner for Refugees [UNHCR] (1993) *The State of the World's Refugees: the Challenge of Protection* London: Penguin

United Nations High Commissioner for Refugees [UNHCR] (1994) *Refugee Children: Guidelines on Protection and Care* Geneva: UNHCR

US Committee for Refugees (1996) *World Refugee Survey 1996* Washington DC: US Committee for Refugees

Utting, W. (1991) *Children in the Public Care* London: HMSO

Van der Veer, G. (1992) *Counselling and Therapy with Refugees: Psychological Problems of Victims of War, Torture and Repression* Chichester: John Wiley and Sons

Van der Veer, G. (1995) 'Psychotherapeutic work with refugees.' in Kleber, R., Figley, C. and Gersons, B. (Eds) *Beyond Trauma: Cultural and Societal Dynamics.* New York: Plenum Press

Wagner, P. and Lodge, C. (1995). *Refugee Children in School* Staff development materials from NAPCE

Warner, R. (Ed.). (1995) *Voices from ....* London: Minority Rights Group

Wicks, B. (1989) *The Day They Took the Children.* London: Bloomsbury

Williams, R., Joseph, S and Yule, W. (1993) 'Disaster and mental health.' In Leff, J. and Bhugra, D. (Eds). *Principles of Social Psychiatry.* Oxford: Blackwell Scientific. pp 450-469.

Williamson, J. and Moser, A. (1987) *Unaccompanied Children in Emergencies: A Field Guide for their Care and Protection.* Geneva: International Social Service

Wolf. A. (1994) *Parity of Esteem: Can Vocational Awards Ever Achieve High Status?* London: Institute of Education, University of London.

World Health Organization (1994) *International Classification of Diseases: 10th Edition* (ICD-10). Geneva: WHO

Young Minds (1994) *War and Refugee Children: the Effects of War on Child Mental Health* London: The National Association for Child and Family Mental Health

Yule, W. (1991) 'Work with children following disasters' in Herbert, M. (ed) *Clinical Child Psychology: Social Learning, Development and Behaviour* Chichester: John Wiley. pp 349-363

Yule, W. (1992a) 'Post traumatic stress disorder in child survivors of shipping disasters: The sinking of the 'Jupiter'' *Psychotherapy and Psychosomatics, 57,* 200-205

Yule, W. (1992b) 'Resilience and vulnerability in child survivors of disasters' in Tizard, B. and Varma, V. (Eds) *Vulnerability and Resilience: A Festschrift for Ann and Alan Clarke.* London: Jessica Kingsley. pp 82-98

Yule, W. (1994) 'Post Traumatic Stress Disorders' in Ollendick, T.H., King, N. and Yule, W. (eds) *Handbook of Phobic and Anxiety Disorders of Children.* New York: Plenum Press.

Yule, W., Bolton, D. and Udwin, O. (1992) *Objective and subjective predictors of PTSD in adolescents.* Paper presented at World Conference of International Society for Traumatic Stress Studies, "Trauma and Tragedy", Amsterdam, 21-26 June, 1992.

Yule, W. and Gold, A. (1993) *Wise Before the Event: Coping with Crises in Schools.* London: Calouste Gulbenkian Foundation.

Yule, W. and Udwin, O. (1991) 'Screening child survivors for post-traumatic stress disorders: Experiences from the 'Jupiter' sinking.' *British Journal of Clinical Psychology,* 30, 131-138.

Yule, W., Udwin, O. and Murdoch, K. (1990) 'The 'Jupiter' sinking: Effects on children's fears, depression and anxiety.' *Journal of Child Psychology and Psychiatry,* 31, 1051-1061.

Yule, W. and Williams, R. (1990) 'Post traumatic stress reactions in children.' *Journal of Traumatic Stress,* 3 (2) , 279-295

Zealey, C. (1995) 'The importance of names' in The National Early Years Network *The Co-ordinate Collection: Equal Opportunities* London: The National Early Years Network.

Index

Admission to school 6, 7, 37, 38, 45-46,
   108, 130-134, 143-145, 158-159, 163,
   168, 174, 180, 181
Angolan refugees 120-121
Asylum and Immigration Act 1996 4, 20,
   26, 27, 30, 36, 50, 65, 114, 123, 127
Asylum and Immigration (Appeals) Act
   1993 20, 26, 27, 36, 50, 55
Asylum procedures 14-16

Basque children 21, 51, 73
Belgian refugees 21
Bilingualism 96, 99, 100, 114-115

Children Act 1989 30-31, 50, 61-63, 68, 70
Conflict resolution 17
Czechoslovakian refugees 22

Demographic data 2, 5, 13-15, 23, 52-55,
   64, 108, 173
Department for Education and
   Employment 70, 133, 175
Department of Health 63, 70-71, 72, 74
Detention 55

Early years provision 93-105
Education Reform Act 1988 126, 152
English as an additional language 6-9, 97-
   99, 114, 135-136, 151, 156, 157, 162,
   164-166, 169, 176, 178, 181
Eritrean refugees 104, 109, 125, 147, 167
European harmonisation 25-27, 32

Foster care 66-67
Friendship patterns 43-44
Further education 134, 140, 152-170
Further and Higher Education Act 1993
   152

GEST 8, 129-130, 181
global curriculum 73, 99-102, 115, 136-
   138, 177-178
Health conditions 25, 31, 40-41
Home/school liaison 48, 96, 121-122, 128,
   176
Housing 4, 29, 30, 33-48
   and temporary accommodation 28,
   30, 34, 39, 42-43, 45, 47, 65
Housing Act 1996 35, 36
Hungarian refugees 22, 52

Jewish refugees 21, 51-52, 73, 172

Kurdish refugees 1,2, 93, 103, 125, 145

Local authority policy 47-48, 74, 63-69,
   104-105, 146
Local Authority Social Services Act 1970
   70

Pastoral care in schools 48, 73-74, 90-92,
   112-113, 118-119, 146, 163-164, 178,
   181
Play 97-98
Polish refugees 21
Post Traumatic Stress Disorder 77-82, 88,
   89, 90, 116, 141-142
Psychological adaption 9, 23-25, 26, 31,
   46, 75-92, 95-96, 99-100, 108-113,
   126-127, 140-142, 177
   and crisis intervention 85-88, 118
   protective factors 83-85, 111-113,
   141
   risk factors 83-85, 111-113, 141
Public expenditure 19

Racism 9, 18, 19, 20, 29-30, 174
Refugee community organisations 112,
    113, 128, 174, 179, 181
Refugee support teachers 10, 107-108
Rwanda 17

School policy 48, 72-74, 129-132, 134
Section 11 of 1966 Local Government Act
    8, 10, 11, 156, 175
Somali refugees 58, 103, 104, 108, 109,
    119, 125, 137-138, 139, 157-158

Tamil refugees 20, 108, 125, 158

Unaccompanied refugee children 49-74
    and Panel of Advisers 55, 57, 65

UN Convention Relating to the Status of
    Refugees 13-14, 20, 31, 49, 60, 76
UN Convention on the Rights of the Child
    49
UNHCR 57

Vietnamese refugees 22, 52, 94, 97, 102

War 16-18, 50, 57, 75-76, 82, 84, 127
Welfare benefits 26, 27, 30, 65, 160

Yugoslavia 18, 27, 31, 52, 55, 9, 172
    and conflict in Bosnia 75, 82

Zaire (Republic of Congo) 108, 116-118,
    135